Expositions

Weekly Lessons and Meditations for Believers

by

Ronald B. Davis

Millennium International
Publishing Group

Cover photograph Copyright © 2021 by Ronald B. Davis
Cover design by Millennium International Publishing Group, LLC
Publishing services provided by Millennium International Publishing Group, LLC

FOREWORD

Since coming to Allen Chapel, Daytona Beach in 2007, I have had the privilege of knowing Brother Ronald B. Davis in his capacity as a member of the church, class leader of class number (1) and vice chair of the Board of Stewards. He has demonstrated maturity in handling the word of God and consistency in his personal spiritual growth. I am excited that he has chosen to put in journal form, expositions that he shared, that were birthed from the "I Believe" prayer line.

I have come to discover that people generally fall into one of these three groups in life: the few who make things happen, the many who watch things happen, and the overwhelming majority who have no notion of what happens. Every person is either a creator of fact or a creature of circumstance. He either puts color into his environment, or, like a chameleon, takes color from his environment. Or to put it another way: Some people are thermometers; they conform completely to their environment – their behavior is determined from without. Other people are thermostats. Instead of allowing their environment to control them, they determine the environment.

As you begin this journey of reading and reflecting on the content of this journal, decide for yourself the best time of the day for your prayer and reflection and be disciplined enough to stick to your schedule to have a real encounter with the Holy Spirit. Although you may hope for a deeply moving experience each day, you cannot expect to be touched by every reading or exposition. In fact, some days you may find yourself being distracted or critical of what is written. Other times you might wonder why in the world you are spending your time this way. But, if you stay with your commitment, you will discover your life is slowly and gently being transformed by your willingness to spend regular time with your loving God.

Rev. Dr. Nathan M. Mugala

Table of Contents

Pray According to His Will

1 John 5:14-15 (NKJV)

[14] Now this is the confidence that we have in Him, that if we ask anything according to His will, He hears us. [15] And if we know that He hears us, whatever we ask, we know that we have the petitions that we have asked of Him.

In this passage, John begins to offer some concluding remarks and applications of the teaching of his first epistle. Having told us how we might find assurance of salvation, the apostle gives us a few final exhortations before he lays down his pen.

Verse 14 returns to the subject of having confidence before God that John spoke of in chapter 3:21, which says, "Beloved, if our heart does not condemn us, we have confidence toward God." We saw then that when we are assured of our salvation we gain confidence before God, confidence that makes us obey His will and thus receive from Him what we request. True assurance produces obedience, and obedience results in us seeing answered prayer in accordance with God's will.

If you read 1 John chapter 3:21 you will be careful to note that our obedience is not necessarily the cause of God's affirmative responses to prayer, nor does it ensure it. We know God only says yes to our prayers when we pray according to His will. Therefore, obedience is linked to such answered prayer in that those who obey God know His will and therefore pray in line with His will much of the time.

It is 1 John chapter 5:14 that tells us explicitly God "hears us." God answers our prayers in the affirmative when we pray according to His will. Verse 15 also tells us that if we know God hears us, then we can know we will have our requests granted. In other words, both verses give us confidence that anything asked for in accordance with God's will shall be done.

In one sense this can go without saying since the Bible uniformly asserts that God's will is always done. For example, Job 42:2 reads,

1

"I know that You can do everything, And that no purpose *of Yours* can be withheld from You." Why, then, do we pray?

First, we pray because we are commanded to do so (Matt. 6:5–15). God tells us to pray, and since He is our Lord, we must do so.

Secondly, we know that though God's will is always done, He often uses us to accomplish His will. God ordains our prayers and uses them as a powerful means to bring about the ends He has also decreed. We do not know what God has ordained, but we do know He uses our prayers to bring about His ends. As we pray according to His will, He uses us as tools to execute His purposes.

God's will is always accomplished, and we must remember that our prayers are meaningfully used by God to bring about His purposes. God has decided to use us to accomplish His ordained ends, and this privilege should move us to seek His will so we might pray properly and effectually. Spend some time in prayer today asking God to help you understand and pray His will at all times.

Prayer is not optional for God's children; it is essential. If you do not pray, you are not living by faith in God. If you do not pray, you are trusting in yourself, which is exactly how the world lives.

1.   We should have confidence when we approach God in prayer.

Our confidence is never in ourselves, but rather in Christ. After reminding us of our sympathetic high priest, the author of Hebrews states (4:16), "Therefore let us draw near with confidence to the throne of grace, so that we may receive mercy and find grace to help in time of need" (see also, Eph. 3:12). Our confidence is never in ourselves, but only in Jesus Christ whose blood gives us access to the very throne of God.

2.   We must come into His presence when we pray.

We have confidence *before Him* (1 John 5:14). Prayer is not just mumbling through a list or repeating some rote formula. Prayer is coming before the living God, humbling ourselves in His presence. If we have not come before God, we haven't prayed.

3. We must come confidently into His presence and ask.

As James 4:2 reminds us, "You do not have because you do not ask." He adds (4:3), "You ask and do not receive, because you ask with wrong motives, so that you may spend it on your pleasures." We need to be sure to ask (not assume), but we need to ask with the proper motives, that our requests would further God's purpose and glory.

4. If we ask anything according to His will, He hears us.

Since God hears everything and even knows the unspoken secrets of our hearts, John means that He hears us favorably by coming to our aid. Our heavenly Father knows the cries of His children. He hears our prayers.

5. If we know that He hears us, "we know that we have the requests which we have asked from Him" (1 John 5:15).

The idea of verse 15 is to know that we presently have whatever we have asked in accord with His will. We may not actually see it for many years, but it's as good as done. Abraham prayed for a son and God promised to give him that son. But it was 25 years before Abraham held Isaac in his arms. Sometimes in His purpose and wisdom, God delays the answers to our prayers for years. Yet, in another sense, He has already granted the requests.

You don't have to continue praying for the same thing over and over; however, there is nothing wrong with continuing to pray until the request is granted (Luke 18:1-8). You can begin thanking God even though you haven't yet received what you were praying for because if you are praying God's will you know it's going to happen.

Biblical prayer is not trying to talk God into giving us what we want. Rather, it is submitting our will to His will. It is praying, as Jesus instructed, "Your will be done, on earth as it is in heaven" (Matthew 6:10).

Immerse yourself in the written Word of God; saturate your mind with it. And pray that the Spirit of Christ will make you so new that the spillover will be good, acceptable, and perfect to the will of God. The Will of God won't take you where the Grace of God can't protect you.

Always remember: If God takes you to it, God will bring you through it. We serve an awesome God!

Notes: _____

_____

_____

_____

_____

_____

_____

_____

_____

_____

_____

_____

_____

_____

_____

_____

_____

_____

_____

_____

Praying in the Spirit

Ephesians 6:18-20 (NLT)

[18]Pray in the Spirit at all times and on every occasion. Stay alert and be persistent in your prayers for all believers everywhere. [19]And pray for me, too. Ask God to give me the right words so I can boldly explain God's mysterious plan that the Good News is for Jews and Gentiles alike. [20]I am in chains now, still preaching this message as God's ambassador. So pray that I will keep on speaking boldly for him, as I should.

What exactly does it mean to pray in the Spirit? Praying in the Spirit is mentioned three times in Scripture. 1 Corinthians 14:15 reads, "Well then, what shall I do? I will pray in the spirit, and I will also pray in words I understand. I will sing in the spirit, and I will also sing in words I understand." Ephesians 6:18 reads, "And pray in the Spirit on all occasions with all kinds of prayers and requests. With this in mind, be alert and always keep on praying for all the saints." Jude 1: 20 reads, "But you, dear friends, build yourselves up in your most holy faith and pray in the Holy Spirit."

Praying in the Spirit does not refer to the words we are saying. Rather, it refers to how we are praying. Praying in the Spirit is praying according to the Spirit's leading. It is praying for things the Spirit leads us to pray for. Sometimes in life, we are so overwhelmed we don't even know what we should pray for. Romans 8:26 tells us, "In the same way, the Spirit helps us in our weakness. We do not know what we ought to pray for, but the Spirit Himself intercedes for us with groans that words cannot express."

God understands the words contained in even a single tear, but we can achieve nothing by allowing our soul to vent by crying. We need to take God's hand and pray in the Spirit.

Praying in the Spirit has many benefits. For one, the fruit of the Spirit is released in us, which has supernatural effects on our attitudes and personality. They are given off by Him resting in us and on us. Aside from this practical and necessary benefit, praying in the Spirit gives us specific, unique advantages that we achieve by allowing the Spirit to pray through us.

Praying in the Spirit gives us wisdom, gives us even more of an advantage in spiritual warfare, and causes us to be "built up" and edified in our spirit man. When we pray in the Spirit, the Spirit of God intercedes for us according to whatever God's will is. The Spirit searches all things, even the deep things of God. Since the Spirit of God searches our hearts, He finds and thoroughly knows what we long for in our hearts that we can't even begin to articulate. What's more, He cares. The Spirit of God also knows His will for our lives. God's Spirit pulls together our heart's desires, God's will aligns them, and the Spirit prays for that alignment to come to pass!

If we are desiring something that really isn't God's best for us, then the Spirit can align our hearts so that we do desire His highest and best for our lives. We don't have to be afraid of God's will. His commands are not grievous and He loves us with a perfect love. The Spirit of God uses wisdom to pray for what we need to, He aligns our hearts with God's, and He also prays for those things we're longing for.

When we are in Spiritual Warfare, Satan cannot understand what you are praying for when you pray in the Spirit. This gives you the upper hand. Praying in the Spirit means communicating directly with God and no one can understand the mysteries you are praying. When you pray in the Spirit, you are pulling out the big guns!

1 Corinthians 14:2-5 and 14:14-15 read: [2]For he who speaks in a tongue does not speak to men but to God, for no one understands him; however, in the spirit he speaks mysteries. [3]But he who prophesies speaks edification and exhortation and comfort to men. [4]He who speaks in a tongue edifies himself, but he who prophesies edifies the church. [5]I wish you all spoke with tongues, but even more that you prophesied; for he who prophesies is greater than he who speaks with tongues, unless indeed he interprets, that the church may receive edification. [14]For if I pray in a tongue, my spirit prays, but my understanding is unfruitful. [15]What is the conclusion then? I will pray

with the spirit, and I will also pray with the understanding. I will sing with the spirit, and I will also sing with the understanding.

These verses are saying that in our repertoire of spiritual warfare, praying in the Spirit has a very important place, along with prophesying and prayer in our earthly language that people can understand. This verse also says outright that praying in the Spirit is the same as praying in tongues, and that praying in the Spirit edifies you and builds you up. Like an indestructible house that still stands when the storm comes, we should pray in the Spirit to build up our spiritual "walls."

In Psalms, David says he encouraged himself in the Lord. Does that mean he prayed in the Spirit? We don't know. However, many theologians feel that Hannah was praying in the Spirit in 1 Samuel 1:13: "Her lips moved, but no sound was heard, and the man of God, Eli, mistakenly thought she was drunk."

Hannah was in such distress that she didn't know what she should pray for. She was being attacked mentally, emotionally, and spiritually. She needed a way to pray directly to God without Satan being able to intercept what she was saying and hinder her any further. Hannah also had been torn down as a person, a woman, and even as a wife. She desperately needed to be built back up, so her method was to use all the advantages of praying in the Spirit to the maximum.

The Spirit prayed through Hannah because she was unable to find the words. Her heart's desire was for a child, and God's will was to give her one. That's why we don't ever need to be afraid to give our desires to God. If God ever tells us no, it is only because He has something better. Hannah asked specifically for a boy and she received one. The promises of God are yes and amen. All who ask receive; who seek, find; and who knock, it is opened to them!

Samuel M. Zwemer, wrote, "True prayer is God the Holy Spirit talking to God the Father in the name of God the Son, and the believer's heart is the prayer room."

We need to use the arsenal of resources God has equipped us with to go forward in victory! It is vital that we spend time praying in the Spirit so we can be illuminated, adjusted, empowered, edified, and built back up. Life will throw curveballs at us sometimes, and we need to use the powerful weapon of allowing the Spirit to move through us to get us the victory!

Prayer is our greatest Christian privilege, but we fail more in our prayer life than any other place. We're in a battle with the world, the flesh, and the devil - three enemies who don't want us to pray. God knows this, so He has given us Someone to help us in our prayer life—and that Someone is the Holy Spirit. The Holy Spirit of God will help you in your prayer life.

The Holy Spirit is the Source and Sustainer of our spiritual life. "If we live by the Spirit, let us also walk by the Spirit" (Galatians. 5:25). Since prayer is represented in Scripture as an essential factor in progress in the Christian life, it is not surprising to find that the Spirit of God is deeply involved.

You may be where Hannah was before she began to use the weapon of praying in the Spirit. Some of you are in a state of despair, exhaustion, confusion, and fatigue. I hope that you look at Hannah's testimony and use the tools she did to regain the victory and rebuild your life. May God bless you richly as you go forth, whole and complete, nothing missing and nothing broken.

Notes: _____

_____

_____

_____

_____

What Are You Sowing?

Galatians 6:7-10 (NIV)

[7]Do not be deceived: God cannot be mocked. A man reaps what he sows. [8]Whoever sows to please their flesh, from the flesh will reap destruction; whoever sows to please the Spirit, from the Spirit will reap eternal life. [9]Let us not become weary in doing good, for at the proper time we will reap a harvest if we do not give up. [10]Therefore, as we have opportunity, let us do good to all people, especially to those who belong to the family of believers.

To mock God is to disrespect, dishonor, or ignore Him. It is a serious offense committed by those who have no fear of God or who deny His existence. The most easily recognized form of mockery is disrespect, typified by verbal insults or other acts of disdain. It is associated with ridicule, scoffing, and defiance. Mockery is a dishonoring attitude that shows low estimation, contempt, or even open hostility.

In a very real sense, any person who disregards the Word of God saying that they don't believe in God or his Word, and fails to accept the fact that Jesus, the son of God, died on the cross to pay the penalty for their sins, and in so doing rejects God's gift of salvation, forgiveness, and eternal life, is living a life of mockery. This is because they play the role of God in choosing to believe their own word instead of God's Word. Putting themselves above God is not only a mockery, but also a fatal path to follow—eternally fatal.

God has given us his Word and specific warning about life after death, so don't mock God and hope for the best when you come to the end of life's journey. The reality is that we cannot mock God. We will reap what we sow.

Scripture warns us not to be deceived (1 Corinthians. 6:9; 15:33). We can be deceived in many ways, but one of the major sources of deception is self. We find ways to avoid facing unpleasant truths and rationalize away personal guilt. It is foolish to try to deceive ourselves. Galatians 6:7-9 touches on some common illusions among those who profess to be Christians. Sadly, those who try to deceive themselves and others somehow think God will, likewise, be deceived by them.

God Cannot Be Mocked

God is not mocked in that His law cannot be ignored without punishment. Adam and Eve tried it to their sorrow; Ananias and Sapphira tried it to their death. Achan concealed his sin from others, but God was not mocked (Josh. 7). Gehazi, Elisha's servant, tried to gain a personal profit by lying, but God was not mocked (2 Kings 5:20-27). Jonah tried to run from Him, but God would not be mocked.

God is not mocked in that He cannot be deceived. Hebrews. 4:12-13 (NIV) reads: [12]For the word of God is alive and active. Sharper than any double-edged sword, it penetrates even to dividing soul and spirit, joints and marrow; it judges the thoughts and attitudes of the heart. [13]Nothing in all creation is hidden from God's sight. Everything is uncovered and laid bare before the eyes of him to whom we must give account.

We reap what we sow, and we reap in greater quantities than we sow. When the farmer sows wheat, he reaps wheat, sometimes thirtyfold, sixtyfold, or a hundredfold.

God's Law of Harvest Cannot Be Broken

If one sows to the spirit, he has real hope of eternal life. 2 Timothy 4:6-8 says, "For I am already being poured out like a drink offering, and the time for my departure is near. [7]I have fought the good fight, I have finished the race, I have kept the faith. [8]Now there is in store for me the crown of righteousness, which the Lord, the righteous Judge, will award to me on that day—and not only to me, but also to all who have longed for his appearing."

If one is sowing to the flesh, be ready to reap corruption (Romans 3:8; 6:23). We cannot neglect God's law without consequences (Hebrews 2:2-3). We cannot sow the "works of the flesh" and reap heaven (Galatians 5:17-21). We cannot engage in such things as adultery, fornication, uncleanness, lewdness, idolatry, sorcery, hatred, contentions, jealousies, outbursts of wrath, selfish ambitions, dissensions, envy, murders, drunkenness, and the like because those who practice such things will not inherit the kingdom of God. We cannot sow what some call "wild oats" and expect to reap that which is good.

All the Fruits of Our Behavior Are Not Immediate

As a matter of fact, we must look primarily beyond the present for reward. Paul said, "For I consider that the sufferings of this present time are not worthy to be compared with the glory which shall be revealed in us" (Romans 8:18). He added, "For our light affliction, which is but for a moment, is working for us a far more exceeding and eternal weight of glory" (1 Corinthians. 4:17). We should never mistake God's present tolerance for a full harvest.

Some were erroneously thinking that way in New Testament times. The apostle Peter corrected them by saying, "The Lord is not slack concerning His promise, as some count slackness, but is longsuffering toward us, not willing that any should perish but that all should come to repentance. But the day of the Lord will come as a thief in the night, in which the heavens will pass away with a great noise, and the elements will melt with fervent heat; both the earth and the works that are in it will be burned up" (2 Peter. 3:9-10).

The young may escape the wrath of their parents, the law and society, but they will not escape God's judgment. The worldly may think they have "gotten away with sin" if they receive no immediate penalty, or if their sin is condoned by brethren, but such is not the case.

It is easy for us as believers to point the finger at those outside the church who mock God. But the subtlest mockery of God, and the most dangerous, comes from those of us sitting in church. We are guilty of mockery when we behave with an outward show of spirituality or godliness without an inward engagement or change of heart.

The Bible shows us the way to live a blessed life, sometimes by the good examples of godly men and women and sometimes by the negative examples of those who choose to follow another path. Psalm 1:1–3 says, "Blessed is the man who walks not in the counsel of the ungodly, nor stands in the path of sinners, nor sits in the seat of the scornful; ²But his delight is in the law of the LORD, And in His law he meditates day and night. ³He shall be like a tree, planted by the rivers of water, that brings forth its fruit in its season, whose leaf also shall not wither; And whatever he does shall prosper."

Although it is true in a general sense that we reap whatever we sow, it should be noted that this reminder follows an exhortation on Christian giving. Viewed in that light, we see that sowing to the flesh means spending one's money on oneself, one's own pleasures and comforts. Sowing to the spirit is using one's money for the furtherance of God's interests.

Those who do the former reap a harvest of disappointment and loss right here on earth because they learn, as they grow older, that the flesh they live to please is decaying and dying. Then, in the age to come they lose eternal rewards.

Those who sow to the Spirit enjoy eternal life here and now in a way which other Christians do not. Then too, they will reap the rewards, which accompany faithfulness when they reach their heavenly home.

Have you ever really thought about what Jesus sowed? He sowed love, compassion, healing, salvation, truth, grace, goodness, mercy, wisdom, authority, faithfulness, generosity, trust, loyalty, humility, and obedience, and bore all our sins upon Himself.

What He reaped from the world was crucifixion, betrayal, pain, suffering, rejection, judgement, hate, and mocking. He was beaten, deserted, accused, lied about, and doubted.

Is this, then, also our price here on earth for sowing Jesus?

Jesus said, "Whoever wants to be my disciple must deny themselves and take up their cross and follow me."

All of us must realize that God will not be mocked – neither in this life nor in eternity. He is not fooled by our clever deceptions. We will reap what we sow. Therefore, we must obey God.

Notes: _____

_____

_____

_____

_____

_____

_____

_____

_____

_____

_____

_____

_____

_____

_____

_____

_____

_____

_____

_____

_____

_____

_____

_____

Prayer Changes Things

Hezekiah 20:1-6 (NKJV)

[1]In those days Hezekiah was sick and near death. And Isaiah the prophet, the son of Amoz, went to him and said to him, "Thus says the LORD: 'Set your house in order, for you shall die, and not live.'" [2]Then he turned his face toward the wall, and prayed to the LORD, saying, [3]"Remember now, O LORD, I pray, how I have walked before You in truth and with a loyal heart, and have done *what was* good in Your sight." And Hezekiah wept bitterly. [4]And it happened, before Isaiah had gone out into the middle court, that the word of the LORD came to him, saying, [5]"Return and tell Hezekiah the leader of My people, 'Thus says the LORD, the God of David your father: I have heard your prayer, I have seen your tears; surely I will heal you. On the third day you shall go up to the house of the LORD. [6]And I will add to your days fifteen years.'"

Hezekiah was one of the few kings of Judah who was constantly aware of God's acts in the past and His involvement in the events of every day. The Bible describes Hezekiah as a king who had a close relationship with God, one who did "what was good and right and faithful before the LORD his God" (2 Chronicles 31:20).

Because King Hezekiah put God first in everything he did, God prospered him. Hezekiah "held fast to the Lord and did not stop following him; he kept the commands the Lord had given Moses. And the Lord was with him; he was successful in whatever he undertook" (2 Kings 18:6-7).

Get alone with God, spread your problems out before Him honestly, humbly, and boldly; then allow His will to be done as you wait for His response.

God, faithful as always, kept His promise to protect Jerusalem. "That night the angel of the Lord went out and put to death a hundred and eighty-five thousand in the Assyrian camp. When the people got up the next morning—there were all the dead bodies!" (2 Kings 19:35). The remaining Assyrians quickly broke camp and withdrew in abject defeat. "So the Lord saved Hezekiah and the people of Jerusalem... He took care of them on every side" (2 Chronicles 32:22).

Later, Hezekiah became very sick. Isaiah told him to set things in order and prepare to die (2 Kings 20:1). But Hezekiah prayed, beseeching God to be merciful and to remember all the good he had done. Before Isaiah had even left the king's house, God told Isaiah to tell Hezekiah that his prayer had been heard and that his life would be extended fifteen years. Isaiah applied a poultice (a soft, usually heated substance that is spread on cloth and then placed on the skin to heal a sore or to reduce pain), and Hezekiah was healed (2 Kings 20:5-7).

Hezekiah ruled over Judah and was a good and faithful king.

Hezekiah often became the target of warring nations. The king of Assyria, which was a much more powerful nation, decided to attempt a takeover of Hezekiah's kingdom. Throughout the stressful time in leadership, Hezekiah consistently used the same battle plan. He went before the Lord in prayer and followed the Lord's commands. Hezekiah relied on prayer to rule his life. This king knew how to pray and he prayed in a way that got results.

At one point, the Assyrian king launched a huge smear campaign against Hezekiah with his own people. It scared all Hezekiah's people to death.

Hezekiah heard about it and went before the Lord. God assured Hezekiah everything would be okay, but the Assyrians wouldn't let up. They kept taunting and taunting, throwing threats towards Hezekiah. They sent a letter by messenger to Hezekiah which said, "The Assyrians are tough and they are coming for you next."

What do you do when you are backed into a corner about to face something bigger than your ability to handle? Well, Hezekiah received the letter with all the threats and began to pray.

We find this account in 2 Kings 19:14-19.

¹⁴Hezekiah received the letter from the messengers and read it. Then he went up to the temple of the LORD and spread it out before the LORD. ¹⁵And Hezekiah prayed to the LORD: "LORD, the God of Israel, enthroned between the cherubim, you alone are God over all the kingdoms of the earth. You have made heaven and earth. ¹⁶Give ear, LORD, and hear; open your eyes, LORD, and see; listen to the words Sennacherib has sent to ridicule the living God. ¹⁷"It is true, LORD, that the Assyrian kings have laid waste these nations and their lands. ¹⁸They have thrown their gods into the fire and destroyed them, for they were not gods but only wood and stone, fashioned by human hands. ¹⁹Now, LORD our God, deliver us from his hand, so that all the kingdoms of the earth may know that you alone, LORD, are God."

What can we learn from listening in as Hezekiah prayed?

Hezekiah got alone with God. There is corporate prayer like we do at church, and there is prayer where a few are gathered, but probably some of the most effective prayer times of your life will be the time you invest alone with God.

Hezekiah's prayer was **immediate.** It wasn't an afterthought. It was prior to making his plans. We are so geared to react that it's hard for us to go first to God. He may be second or third when we are backed into a corner and have no choice, but as a habit we need to make God the first place we turn in our lives.

Hezekiah's prayer was **open and honest**. Hezekiah was transparent before the Lord. I love the imagery here in this prayer story of Hezekiah. He took the letter, went to the house of the Lord, and spread it out before Him. I get this visual image of Hezekiah laying this letter on a table, and saying, "Okay, God, what now? What do I do next?"

Are you in a tough spot right now? You may just need to get some note cards, write down all the things you are struggling with, lay them out on a table, then say, "Okay God, here are my struggles. I can't do anything about them. What now?"

Writing your prayer requests is a great idea for two reasons. First, it helps you remember what to pray for. Second, it helps you to watch as God answers. We get more answers than we realize if we only ask.

Hezekiah's prayer was **honoring, humble and respectful** of who God is. Hezekiah knew his place as king, and he knew God's place in the Kingdom. Hezekiah was king of a nation and that is an important job, yet Hezekiah willingly humbled himself in prayer, because he knew his place before the King of kings.

Hezekiah's prayer was **Bold.** He said, "Give ear, O LORD, and hear; open your eyes, O LORD…" Hezekiah had the kind of relationship with God where it wasn't a surprise when Hezekiah showed up to pray. They talked frequently, probably throughout the day. Because of that relationship, Hezekiah didn't wonder if God would be there when he came before Him. He knew he could ask God to act on his behalf.

The more you grow in your relationship with God, the more your heart will begin to line up with God's heart, and the bolder your prayers can become.

Hezekiah's prayer was **dependent.** In verses 17-18 he prays, "It is true, O LORD, that the Assyrian kings have laid waste these nations and their lands." Hezekiah knew he was out of his league facing the Assyrians. From the way Hezekiah responded to life, however, I don't think it mattered the size of the battle: Hezekiah was going to depend on God.

Hezekiah's prayer was **certain** because it was based on his personal faith and trust in God. In verse 19, Hezekiah prayed, "Now, O LORD our God, deliver us from his hand, so that all kingdoms on earth may know that you alone, O LORD, are God."

You need to understand that faith is always based on the promises of God. Some things God has promised to do, some He hasn't. God has promised to always get glory for Himself and always work things for an ultimate good. He hasn't promised to rid everyone of cancer or to heal every bad relationship. That doesn't mean we shouldn't pray for everything. We don't know His will, but we can't guarantee God to do that which He hasn't promised to do. Sometimes we get upset because God doesn't do something we asked or wanted Him to do, but the fact is, He had never promised to do it.

Hezekiah knew God had promised to save His people. He knew God had placed him in the position of authority over them. He had confidence that God would do what He had promised to do. Hezekiah trusted God to be faithful to His word so he was willing to act in faith.

What situations are you praying about that you know you are helpless to manage on your own and you desperately desire God's answer? Hezekiah had a faith in God that allowed him to pray with confidence. You can have that same faith. Whatever situation you find yourself in, God can handle it. All you have to do is pray and trust God to be faithful to his word. I'm not making this up; it's right there in the Scripture. [5]"...I have heard your prayer, I have seen your tears; surely I will heal you... [6]And I will add to your days fifteen years..." (2 Kings 20:5-6).

When we are able to move our prayers beyond ourselves and to our Kingdom purposes, we offer God more space to move on our behalf.

Before you go to God with your prayer request, give some thought about what you are asking God for - Our time in prayer is more fruitful when it's focused. Then get alone with God, spread your problems out before Him honestly, humbly, and boldly; then, allow His will to be done, as you wait for His response.

Notes: _____

_____

_____

_____

How Effective are Your Prayers?

James 5:15-16 (NKJV)

[15]And the prayer of faith will save the sick, and the Lord will raise him up. And if he has committed sins, he will be forgiven. [16]Confess *your* trespasses to one another, and pray for one another, that you may be healed. The effective, fervent prayer of a righteous man avails much.

The prayer of faith will save the sick. What is the prayer of faith? The prayer of faith is a "prayer that changes things," not people. Too often we try to help someone by praying that they change their behavior. But people do not change against their will. People need to recognize their need for God and to give their life to Him. Once they do that, then God can show them what He wants them to be and give them the ability to change.

The prayer of faith changes circumstances. Anything that can be seen is subject to change and can be affected by a prayer of faith. 2 Corinthians 4:18 reads, "...for the things which are seen [are] temporal; but the things which are not seen [are] eternal." The prayer of faith changes things like physical ailments, lack of wisdom, or your employment status. Through the prayer of faith, you can have healing and health for your body, wisdom for your mind, and even a good job.

Before you get the wrong idea, the prayer of faith is not a magic wand or a genie in a bottle. But the prayer of faith is a tool that we can use to implement God's will in our lives. Through the prayer of faith, we can have the things that God desires for us to have. God desires us to be healthy, wise, and gainfully employed, etc. Although these good things may not be a reality in your life right now, with the prayer of faith, these things that you are hoping for can become reality.

As stated in James 5:16 "The effectual fervent prayer of a righteous man availeth much." (I believe the word "man" means mankind and, therefore, includes women.) There are three elements here that are required for a prayer that "avails much;" that is, a prayer that God will say "Yes" to:

1. The man (person) praying must be righteous.
2. The prayer must be fervent.
3. The prayer must be effective.

Righteousness

The first element of a prayer that avails much is that the man praying must be righteous. Righteousness is a word that is used in religious circles that may be confusing for new believers. However, the term simply means "a condition of being right." (That is, being right with God).

We are right with God when we have surrendered our life and our will to God and accepted the grace (unearned favor) that God offers to us. Matthew 12:50 tells us, "For whosoever shall do the will of my Father which is in heaven, the same is my brother, and sister, and mother." When this is incorporated into your daily life, it will affect every aspect of your thought and behavior. Perfect submission to God's will is a life-long endeavor. But a righteous man is that man whose heart, mind, and body long for that perfect submission.

Fervent Prayer

The second element of a prayer that God will say yes to is that the prayer must be fervent. Fervent means felt very strongly, having or showing very strong feelings. A fervent prayer is one that is heart-felt and taken seriously. A man who goes to God in prayer halfheartedly should not think that his prayer will avail much.

Too often, the ones who are guilty of a lack of seriousness in prayer are those who pray the most. If your prayers have become an empty ritual or a social obligation, then your prayer is not fervent. (Please note that there is a difference between a "social" obligation and the obligation to obey God.) But if your prayer is heart-felt, serious, and in love and obedience to God, then your prayer is fervent.

Praying Effectively

Now, if you are righteous (right with God) and your prayer is fervent (heart-felt and taken seriously), then it must also be effectual in order for it to avail much; that is, in order for God to answer "Yes." If the words of our prayers are ineffective, then we have not given God much to answer. In fact, some prayers are so ineffective I believe God will answer "no" in order to protect us from ourselves.

For example, if I'm praying for a loved one who was diagnosed with terminal cancer, and in my prayer, I say, "Dear God, I ask you to help his cancer," the prayer is not effective because my loved one's cancer does not need any help. It is already killing them. Of course, I wouldn't have meant it that way but that is what was said. In this situation, the prayer would have been effective by asking God to remove the cancer and restore the loved one's health. You can see that it is important to choose your words carefully, so that you are praying for the thing that you actually want.

At other times, we pray ineffective prayers by asking for the wrong things. The Bible says, [2]Yet you do not have because you do not ask. [3]You ask and do not receive, because you ask amiss, that you may spend *it* on your pleasures (James 4:2-3). For example, if you ask God to make you rich so you can have nicer things, your prayer is ineffective. A more effective prayer is to ask God to meet our needs and give us extra so that we can be a blessing to others with our generosity. There is nothing wrong with having nice things, but if our motivation in prayer is greed, then our prayer is ineffective.

If our purpose for praying is based on pride, bitterness, and anger, then our prayer will be ineffective. We should continually examine our motivations so that we are praying prayers that will accomplish God's will rather than our own selfish ambitions.

Elements of Effective Prayer

There are four things that will always make your prayer effective. Those things are:

1. The Word of God.

2. The Name of Jesus.
3. The Holy Spirit.
4. Activated faith.

If these four things are employed properly, your prayer will bring God's will into reality no matter what your need may be.

Word of God

We need to learn God's Word in a manner that results in an understanding of His desires. It is not enough to simply have the ability to quote Scripture (although it is good if you can). When we know His Word, we will know what He wants and how He does things. When we know what He wants and how He does things, we will be able to make our prayers effective because we will be able to ask for the things that God has said He wants.

The Bible says, (1 John 5:14-15) [14]"And this is the confidence that we have in him, that, if we ask any thing according to his will, he heareth us: [15]And if we know that he hears us, whatsoever we ask, we know that we have the petitions that we desired of him." Since we know that God's Word is His will, we can be confident that He will answer "yes" when we base our prayers on His Word.

Name of Jesus

Praying "in the name of Jesus" is a privilege given to believers. But it is far more than simply adding the words to the end of a prayer. When properly understood, the name of Jesus is a powerful tool which will help to make your prayers effective.

Praying a prayer in the name of Jesus is a privilege granted to us by Jesus himself. We know that we can pray "in the name of Jesus" and expect results because Jesus said that we could. John 14: 13-14 says, "And whatsoever ye shall ask in my name, that will I do, that the Father may be glorified in the Son. If ye shall ask any thing in my name, I will do it."

In John 16:23, Jesus says, "And in that day ye shall ask me nothing. Verily, verily, I say unto you, whatsoever ye shall ask the father in my name, he will give it you."

Jesus makes a tremendous statement in verse 23 when he says, "Whatever you ask." Whatever means *whatever*. It covers every area of life. But he adds the condition, "in my name."

It may not be immediately apparent that this is a condition, but when we examine what it means to pray "in his name," we will discover that there are conditions that must be met for a prayer to truly be "in his name."

It should be obvious, then, that our prayer must be in agreement with God's will in order for it to truly be made "in the name of Jesus." Jesus would never pray anything that is contrary to God's desire. Jesus would never pray a greedy or selfish prayer. If we are to pray with his authority and to promote his interests, we must pray like Jesus would pray if he were here.

Holy Spirit

The Holy Spirit plays a vital role in our prayer life. The Holy Spirit can assist us in praying prayers, which God will say "yes" to. We know this because the Holy Spirit will never do anything that would be contrary to God's will. Romans 8:27 reads, "Now He who searches the hearts knows what the mind of the Spirit *is,* because He makes intercession for the saints according to the will of God."

In the Bible, people received the gift of the Holy Spirit after taking action. "Then Peter said unto them, Repent, and be baptized every one of you in the name of Jesus Christ for the remission of sins, and ye shall receive the gift of the Holy Ghost" (Acts 2:38). They took action; they repented and were baptized. Also, "When they heard [this,] they were baptized in the name of the Lord Jesus. And when Paul had laid [his] hands upon them, the Holy Ghost came on them; and they spake with tongues, and prophesied" (Acts 19:5). Again, they took action, they repented, and Paul laid his hands on them. In both of these passages, it is clear that action was taken before these people received the gift and benefits of the Holy Spirit.

The same is true with you. The knowledge that the Holy Spirit can help you with your prayer is not enough. Action is required on your part. You must take action in order to begin receiving the benefits that the Holy Spirit offers.

Activated Faith

You can activate your faith simply by trusting God. By not only saying, "I believe," but by acting like you believe. God wants us to trust him like Peter did when God asked him to walk on the water. Have enough faith to know he won't let you drown.

The Bible states in Deuteronomy 31:8: "The Lord himself goes before you and will be with you; he will never leave you nor forsake you. Do not be afraid; do not be discouraged." And Jesus Himself said in John 14:1, "Don't let your hearts be troubled. Trust in God, and trust in me."

So, the next time life's circumstances occur, activate your faith by trusting God. Pray to God for wisdom regarding your situation. No matter the challenge you face, trust that God is with you, and by faith, be confident that He will see you through.

Notes: _____

_____

_____

_____

_____

_____

_____

_____

_____

_____

One Day at a Time

Matthew 6:33-34 (NKJV)

But seek first the kingdom of God and his righteousness, and all these things shall be added to you. [34]Therefore, do not worry about tomorrow, for tomorrow will worry about its own things. Sufficient for the day is its own trouble.

Proverbs 27:1 (NIV)

Do not boast about tomorrow, for you do not know what a day may bring.

I'm sure most of us, if not all of us, have heard the song "One Day at a Time:"

One day at a time, sweet Jesus - That's all I'm asking from you - Just Give me the strength - to do every day what I have to do - Yesterday's gone sweet Jesus - And tomorrow may never be mine - Lord Help me today - Show me the way - One day at a time. Do you remember, when you walked among men, - Well Jesus you know, when you're looking below - it's worse now than then. There's pushing and shoving - they are crowding my mind - Lord for my sake, teach me to take, One day at a time.

When I was very young, I thought I would live forever. I mean fifty or sixty years was so far away. Now, here I am. Now the years seem like yesterday.

Life is such a fragile, precious gift. It's something we take for granted every day. It's so easy to assume that tomorrow is our *right* and not a privilege. But the reality is that it's a gift and it can be taken in a flash. Life should be cherished, not just in the moments that bring us happiness, but the ones which also break us because all of them are a gift. All are better than the alternative.

Roman stoic philosopher Seneca suggests that we **"Begin at once to live and count each separate day as a separate life."**

At times, it seemed as though life contained an endless supply of days, especially when I was young.

I never thought about not planning for tomorrow because I knew that I would always have tomorrow. It didn't matter how long I held a grudge or how long I waited to do something I wanted to do; there would be an unlimited pool of other opportunities. At least, that's what I thought back then.

Maybe it's a rite of passage from childhood to adulthood, the moment when you realize life happens now and that's all you're guaranteed. It doesn't really hit you when you merely know it intellectually, like you know your ABCs, state capitals, and other concrete facts.

It hits you when somehow you feel it. Your health declines. You lose someone you love. A tragedy rocks your world. It isn't until you realize that all life fades that you consider *now* a commodity, and a scarce one at that.

But maybe that's irrelevant. Maybe living a meaningful, passionate life has nothing to do with its length and everything to do with its width. **What can you do about it?**

1. Live in the moment. Forget the past and don't concern yourself with the future.
2. Fully embrace the now, no matter what the situation.
3. Do the things you love.
4. Learn to forgive and embrace unconditional love.
5. Live every day as if it's your last, because one day it will be.
6. Believe in "live and let live."
7. Use quiet reflection, honesty, and laughter. Laughter is good for the soul.
8. Be other-centered instead of self-centered.
9. Embrace each experience as if it's your first.

10. Focus on today and how you can do your best to live it to the fullest.

11. Participate in life instead of just watching it pass you by.

12. Stay healthy, eat right, and most importantly, be kind to everyone.

13. Pray, forgive yourself, appreciate others, listen to your gut, do things you enjoy, and remind yourself that we are all loved and connected.

14. Don't sweat the small stuff.

15. Question everything, keep it simple, and help whenever and however you can.

16. Try to enjoy every minute of every day.

17. Appreciate life's every second.

18. Step through new doors. Most of the time, there's something fantastic on the other side.

19. Remember that all is a gift, but the most precious of all gifts is life and love.

20. Keep your spirit free, be flexible, let go.

21. Do one thing every day that scares you.

22. Don't attach to outcomes.

23. Spend as much time with children as possible. They are our future.

24. Enjoy each and every moment of life. Every day is a new challenge and opportunity to discover something new.

25. Travel. It is always an adventure! You get to enjoy what fate has to offer with limited means.

26. Be honestly thankful for every breath you take.

27. Just be.

28. Trust yourself. Trust your own strengths.

29. Pause momentarily before everything you do so that you notice everything you should or could notice.

30. Follow your hopes and not your fears. "But **seek first His kingdom and His righteousness**, and all these things will be added to you. So, **do not worry about tomorrow**…" (Matthew 5:33).

When we have this commitment, we rise above worry. All we care about is doing our best today and serving God as He commands. We let God deal with tomorrow, as we focus on doing everything we can for the cause of His kingdom.

So, with our lives centered on God, unencumbered from stresses that weigh down the world, we excel in every facet of life -- as members of the church, in our families, and in our careers.

Don't Be "of Little Faith"

If we believe as we should, we won't worry about tomorrow. We'll live one day at a time, focused on serving God the best we can.

- "But if God so clothes the grass of the field, which is alive today and tomorrow is thrown into the furnace, will He not much more clothe you? **You of little faith!**" (Matthew 6:30)

- Jesus told his disciples if you have faith as small as a mustard seed, you can say to this mountain, 'move from here to there' and it will move; Nothing will be impossible for you.

Some of us have been saved for a long time and we should be beyond just mustard seed faith. So, if we're worried about tomorrow, the problem is with our faith.

We need to increase our faith with the word of God, applying it to our lives, growing and coming to the full knowledge of God (Romans 1:16; 10:17; 2 Peter 1:2-11).

God Knows What You Need, and Will Provide

In commanding us not to worry about tomorrow, Jesus tells us that God knows all our needs, and will supply the necessities of life. If we believe Jesus, we won't worry: "**Do not worry** then, saying, 'What will we eat?' or 'What will we drink?' or 'What will we wear for clothing?' For the Gentiles eagerly seek all these things; **for your heavenly Father knows that you need all these things**" (Matthew 5:31-32).

Just as God takes care of the birds, lilies, and grass, He takes care of us (Matthew 6:26, 28, 30). God knows everything about us, so we don't fear what people may do to us, and don't worry about tomorrow (Matthew 6:26-30; 10:28-39).

Sometimes the problem is that we're afraid to only accept what God gives us, wanting to make sure all our desires are fulfilled. So, we worry about tomorrow, unable to bear the thought of having less than we want, or less than someone else.

Again, this goes to our attitude and commitment. If we're committed to seeking God first, we won't be like unbelievers who are focused on possessions and wealth. As long as we're in a right relationship with God, things of the world won't matter, and we won't worry about tomorrow.

Worry Doesn't Help

Jesus points out the irony of this whole discussion, in that, worry doesn't help. "And **who of you by being worried can add** a single hour to his life" (Matthew. 6:27)? We can't change anything by worrying.

Science confirms that worry decreases performance. Many people spend thousands of dollars on psychologists and life coaches to decrease worry and increase performance. But most of them fail, and worry continues because they aren't approaching it from a biblical perspective.

Worry can *only* be eliminated with a strong faith in God, putting Him first in everything.

As a result, Christians are the most successful people in life, first and foremost in our spiritual lives, and also in our physical lives.

Don't Store Up Treasures on Earth

Immediately before commanding us not to worry, Jesus commands us not to store up treasures on earth, but to store them up in heaven. We can't serve two masters; we'll either hate the one and love the other, or we'll be devoted to one and despise the other (Matthew 6:19-24).

Jesus connects these two teachings, so understanding their relationship is important.

Because God is first in our lives, we aren't worried about tomorrow. So, we're not striving for material wealth, because we're striving to serve God.

In closing, if God blesses us with material wealth, we're happy and content, using our blessings to His glory. But if God doesn't bless us with material wealth, we're just as happy and content, using our blessings in His kingdom. Wealth doesn't matter, just serving God, and working in His kingdom are important.

As Christians, we take life one day at a time.

We don't worry about tomorrow, but are happy and content with our blessings, successful in every aspect of life, because we put God first in everything. The songwriter said it best when he wrote:

"I don't know about tomorrow; I just live from day to day.

I don't borrow from its sunshine, For its skies may turn to grey.

I don't worry o'er the future, For I know what Jesus said.

And today I'll walk beside Him, For He knows what is ahead.

Many things about tomorrow I don't seem to understand,

But I know who holds tomorrow, And I know who holds my hand."

Notes: _____

_____

_____

_____

_____

_____

_____

_____

_____

_____

_____

_____

_____

_____

_____

_____

_____

_____

_____

_____

_____

_____

_____

There is Nothing Too Hard for God

Ezekiel 37:1-6 (NKJV)

¹The hand of the LORD came upon me and brought me out in the Spirit of the LORD, and set me down in the midst of the valley; and it was full of bones. ²Then He caused me to pass by them all around, and behold, there were very many in the open valley; and indeed, they were very dry. ³And He said to me, "Son of man, can these bones live?" So, I answered, "O Lord GOD, You know." ⁴Again He said to me, "Prophesy to these bones, and say to them, 'O dry bones, hear the word of the LORD!' ⁵ Thus says the Lord GOD to these bones: "Surely I will cause breath to enter into you, and you shall live. ⁶ I will put sinews on you and bring flesh upon you, cover you with skin and put breath in you; and you shall live. Then you shall know that I am the LORD."

Most people associate the book of Ezekiel with one of two things: God's chariot with the "wheel in the middle of a wheel," or the dry bones that come back to life.

Ezekiel begins his account with these words: "The hand of the Lord was upon me, and carried me out in the spirit of the Lord, and set me down in the midst of the valley which was full of bones" (Ezekiel 37:1).

Ezekiel's vision of the valley of dry bones (Ezekiel 37:14) came to him after God had directed him to prophesy the rebirth of Israel in chapter 36. God had just announced, through the prophet, that Israel will be restored to her land in blessing under the leadership of "David, My servant [who] shall be king over them" (Ezekiel 37:24), clearly a reference to the future under Jesus Christ the Messiah, descendant of David (Isaiah 7:14, 9:6-7; Luke 1:31-33).

However, this seemed remote, in light of Israel's present condition. She was "dead" as a nation, deprived of her land, her king, and her Temple. She had been divided and dispersed for so long that unification and restoration seemed impossible. So, God gave Ezekiel the vision of the dry bones as a sign. God transported Ezekiel—probably not literally, but in a vision—to a valley full of dry bones and directed him to speak to the bones.

Ezekiel was to tell the bones that God would make breath enter the bones and they would come to life, just as in the creation of man when He breathed life into Adam (Genesis 2:7). Ezekiel obeyed, then in verse seven through verse ten it happened. Suddenly as he spoke, there was a rattling noise all across the valley. The bones of each body came together and attached themselves as complete skeletons. Then muscles, flesh and skin formed over the bones, but they still had no breath in them.

9Then he said to me, "Speak a prophetic message to the winds, son of man. And he said: Come, O breath, from the four winds! Breathe into these dead bodies so they may live again." 10And breath came into their bodies. They all came to life and stood up on their feet—a great army (Ezekiel 37).

In the first vision of verses 1 and 2, Ezekiel saw the dry bones of Israel and Judah in a valley. He was ordered to prophesy to the bones that they would come to life. I believe this makes an application to our need of breath of the life today.

With weirdness, realism, and dramatic force, the prophet presents the heartening news that Israel may hope to live. A revival is possible! Even dry bones without sinew (strong tissue that connects muscles to bones) and flesh and blood, can live.

The coming of God's Spirit brings life. The same thrilling truth is still needed in a world that has dry bones everywhere. What we need is to have the Holy Spirit come with his quickening power that a genuine revival may sweep the earth. The first time he spoke the Word of God, sinews, flesh, and skin came upon the bones.

The next time he prophesied the wind of breath, and the breath came into the bodies. This pictured the national restoration of Israel, first the restoration of the people spiritually dead and then their generation.

This vision symbolized the whole House of Israel that was then in captivity.

Like unburied skeletons, the people were in a state of living death, pining away with no end to their judgment in sight. They thought their hope was gone and they were cut off forever. The surviving Israelites felt their national hopes had been dashed and the nation had died in the flames of Babylon's attack with no hope of resurrection.

The reviving of the dry bones signified God's plan for Israel's future national restoration. The vision also, and most importantly, showed that Israel's new life depended on God's power and not the circumstances of the people. Putting "breath" by God's Spirit in the bones showed that God would not only restore them physically but spiritually as well.

In the vision, God asked Ezekiel a question. He said, "Son of man, can these bones live?" The prophet replied, "O Sovereign LORD, you alone know the answer to that" (verse 3). God knows everything. He doesn't ask us questions because He's been stumped; He asks in order to get us to think. Some teachers teach by asking questions. So, too, God asks people questions in order to arouse their thought processes and to get them to analyze the situation. "Come now, and let us reason together, saith the Lord" (Isaiah 1:18). If Ezekiel had responded to God's question based on the evidence of his senses, he would have answered "no." Dead, dry bones cannot come back to life.

If you were the first to the scene of an accident and you saw somebody lying motionless on the ground, you might think, "Perhaps there's hope." You would probably even do a little CPR and try to revive the person. But if you saw a skeleton lying in the road, you wouldn't even consider giving it mouth-to-mouth resuscitation. You'd think, "It's just dead bones. There's no hope."

Here is the good news that God wants us to learn from this story. There is nothing too hard for God. In a valley of dry bones, what may appear hopeless and dead to you and me is a field full of possibilities for the Lord. Have you known people you thought were too far lost to be found? Someone whom it seemed useless to pray for? The Bible says, never give up! "So let's not get tired of doing what is good. At just the right time we will reap a harvest of blessing, if we don't give up" (Galatians 6:9, NLT).

Nothing is impossible for God. Allow me to share two familiar stories with you.

In Luke 1:26 the angel Gabriel showed up. In verse 31, Gabriel tells Mary she would conceive in her womb and bring forth a Son and shall call his name Jesus. In verse 34, Mary asks, "how can this be since I don't know a man." In verse 35, the angel answered, "The Holy Spirit will come on you, and the power of the Most High will overshadow you. So, the holy one to be born will be called the Son of God." Verse 37 says, "Nothing is impossible with God." And in verse 38, Mary answered, "I am the Lord's servant. May your word to me be fulfilled."

When the Lord was with Abraham, He told him he would return the same time next year and his wife Sarah would have a son. Sarah was in a tent behind Him, overheard the conversation and laughed to herself. She managed to conceal her laughter, but that doesn't work with the Lord, who knows the very thoughts and intentions of our hearts. When the Lord asked, "Why did Sarah laugh?" she denied it and said, "I didn't laugh." But the Lord knew differently and said, "No, but you did laugh." It wasn't a laughing matter to the Lord. The problem was that Sarah's laughter reflected her unbelief in the promise of God. Unbelief is a more serious sin than most of us realize.

God doesn't take kindly to unbelief. To doubt God's promise is equal to calling God a liar. It is to say that I know better than the eternal Creator. It is to demote God from His place of sovereign power and to promote oneself over Him.

All of us struggle, at different levels, with the problem of unbelief. Perhaps, like Abraham and Sarah, you've prayed for something for years, but God has not answered. Life is passing you by while you wait. You struggle with doubt as you often wonder whether He is hearing your prayers. When the disciples asked, "Who then can be saved?" Jesus said, "With men it is impossible, but not with God; for with God all things are possible" (Matthew 19:25-26).

The Bible is saying that without Christ we can't do anything, but through Christ all things are possible. God never wants us to lose faith that He can give life -- even if it appears that a situation is hopeless. We have all heard the proverb "where there is life, there is hope" (Ecclesiastes 9:4). Yet with God, there is even hope when there appears to be no life!

Some of us do a pretty good job of covering up our dry bones. Our dry bones can be marriages, the loss of a loved one, conflict in our families or on our jobs. Some of us have bank accounts that are like dry bones; some of us have health problems. Whatever the case, this message reminds us that God can breathe new life into your dry bones situation.

As I prepared this message, it reminded me that all of us struggle from time to time. If you are not in a storm or if you have never been in a storm, keep living, a storm is coming. That's life.

1. **But remember that your character should always be stronger than your circumstances.** We can't always control what happens to us, but we can always control how we choose to respond. In those moments when I choose to stop complaining and instead give thanks to God for the good in my life, the parts that seem bad start to seem much less significant. Choose to keep a positive attitude and thankful heart, regardless of what you're going through.

   "Rejoice always, pray continually, give thanks in all circumstances; for this is God's will for you in Christ Jesus." (1 Thessalonians 5:16-18)

2. **Remember that your struggles always lead to strength.** Every difficulty in your life, whether big or small, is something God will use to produce more strength, faith, and perseverance in you if you let Him! All your pain has a purpose.

"And we know that in all things God works for the good of those who love him, who have been called according to his purpose." (Romans 8:28)

3. **Remember that God's timing is always perfect.** God's plans are almost always different from our plans, but His plans are always perfect! Have the patience to wait on His timing instead of forcing your own.

   "For I know the plans I have for you declares the Lord; plans to prosper you and not to harm you, plans to give you hope and a future." (Jeremiah 29:11)

4. **Remember that God will never leave your side.** You may feel like you're going through a struggle all alone, but from the moment you ask Jesus to bring you into God's family, He will be by your side until the end, so never lose hope!

So, if you are going through a dry bones situation, pray for that revival today. If you are facing increasing obstacles in your life, lean on God and trust his flawless record, He never fails. He can do the impossible. How do I know? I've seen him do it. Even when your life has gone astray, He'll preserve and cover you with his grace. That's how God works. There is nothing, I repeat, *nothing* too hard for God.

Notes: _____

_____

_____

_____

_____

_____

_____

Examine Yourself

Joel 2:13 (KJV)

[13]And rend your heart, and not your garments, and turn unto the Lord your God: for He is gracious and merciful, slow to anger, and of great kindness, and repenteth him of the evil.

The word of God is calling us to come out of our religious rhetoric and placating piety to convey a message to the body of Christ as well as the world that it's the inside that counts. Enough of just doing, "just to do." Enough of putting on, enough of walking around, looking good on the outside and being torn up on the inside. It's time to get in proper order, rend our heart and not our garments, and turn unto the Lord our God.

By people's standards, Jeremiah was a failure.

Most definitions of success include references to achieving goals and acquiring wealth, prestige, favor, and power. Successful people enjoy the good life, being financially and emotionally secure, surrounded by admirers, and enjoying the fruits of their labors. They are leaders, opinion makers, and trendsetters. Their example is emulated, and their accomplishments are noticed. They know who they are and where they are going, and they stride confidently to meet their goals. By these standards, Jeremiah was a miserable failure.

For 40 years Jeremiah served as God's spokesman to Judah, but when Jeremiah spoke, nobody listened. Consistently and passionately, he urged them to act, but nobody moved. And he certainly did not attain material success. Jeremiah was poor and underwent severe deprivation to deliver his prophecies. He was thrown into prison, and he was taken to Egypt against his will. Jeremiah was rejected by his neighbors, his family, the false priest and prophets, friends, his audience, and the kings. Throughout his life, Jeremiah stood alone, declaring God's message of doom, and announcing the new covenant, and weeping over the fate of his beloved country. In the eyes of the world, Jeremiah was not a success. But in God's eyes, Jeremiah was one of the most successful people in all of history.

Success, as measured by God, involves obedience and faithfulness, regardless of opposition and personal cost.

The people of Judah had become prosperous and complacent. They were taking God for granted. They had turned to self-centeredness, idolatry, and sin. In the beginning of the book, Joel has a message from God for the people of Judah. "Tell your children of your history. Tell them how God has been faithful. Tell them how God has never left you nor forsaken you. Tell them how God has had grace and mercy upon you." Joel declares that the Lord says turn to me now, while there is still time. Give me your hearts. He didn't ask for our money, he didn't ask for our marriages, he didn't ask for our children, he didn't ask for the car, the house, or anything else. God said give me your hearts. Come with fasting, weeping, and mourning.

Isn't it interesting that God asks for the heart before he asks for the fasting, weeping, and mourning? God doesn't want our lip service; he doesn't want our Oscar-winning, Emmy-qualifying, rhetorical religiosity or pretentious pomp and circumstance. God is not interested in the people's choice. It's the inside that counts.

When God has your heart, there's got to be a change.

When God has your heart, there should be a difference.

When God has your heart, there is no second-guessing, there is no hesitation.

If God says go, I'm gone. God says do, it's done. When we examine ourselves, we need to look *through* the person in the mirror to the *heart* of the person in the mirror.

Just ask Noah. It didn't look like rain. It didn't smell like rain. Rain was not in the forecast, but God said build the ark and it was built.

Just ask Shadrach, Meshach, and Abednego. God said thou shalt have no other Gods before thee. King Nebuchadnezzar wanted them to bow to him, but they didn't.

Just ask Job. He lost all that he had and was afflicted in his body. He was dealing with his friends, dealing with his wife, and dealing with life, but he kept on serving God; he kept on believing in God. Job didn't just serve him with lip service, but with everything he had on the inside because everything on the outside was gone.

Moses had a change of heart when he started serving God and stopped making excuses.

Gideon had a change of heart when he stopped hiding on the floor of the winepress thinking he was not good enough.

Jacob had a change of heart when he wrestled with God – I won't let you go until you bless me.

Rahab had a change of heart when she hid the spies.

Joseph had a change of heart when he could have deprived his brothers while there was a famine in Egypt, but he helped them.

Isaiah had a change of heart – here am I Lord, send me.

Peter had a change of heart – at first he denied Jesus, but in the end he deified Him.

The prodigal son changed his heart and came home.

The Samaritan woman at the well changed her heart and drank of the living water.

We need to examine ourselves, beginning with the heart.

May God bless you and keep you is my prayer. Amen.

Notes: _____

_____

_____

_____

_____

Help My Unbelief

Mark 9:14-29 (NKJV)

¹⁴And when He came to the disciples, He saw a great multitude around them, and scribes disputing with them. ¹⁵Immediately, when they saw Him, all the people were greatly amazed, and running to *Him,* greeted Him. ¹⁶And He asked the scribes, "What are you discussing with them?"

¹⁷Then one of the crowd answered and said, "Teacher, I brought You my son, who has a mute spirit. ¹⁸And wherever it seizes him, it throws him down; he foams at the mouth, gnashes his teeth, and becomes rigid. So I spoke to Your disciples, that they should cast it out, but they could not."

¹⁹He answered him and said, "O faithless generation, how long shall I be with you? How long shall I bear with you? Bring him to Me." ²⁰Then they brought him unto Him. And when he saw Him, immediately the spirit convulsed him, and he fell on the ground and wallowed, foaming at the mouth.

²¹So He asked his father, "How long has this been happening to him?"

And he said, "From childhood. ²²And often he has thrown him both into the fire and into the water to destroy him. But if You can do anything, have compassion on us and help us."

²³Jesus said to him, "If you can believe,[a] all things *are* possible to him who believes."

²⁴Immediately the father of the child cried out and said with tears, "Lord, I believe; help my unbelief!"

²⁵When Jesus saw that the people came running together, He rebuked the unclean spirit, saying to it: "Deaf and dumb spirit, I command you, come out of him and enter him no more!" ²⁶Then *the spirit* cried out, convulsed him greatly, and came out of him. And he

became as one dead, so that many said, "He is dead." ²⁷But Jesus took him by the hand and lifted him up, and he arose.

²⁸And when He had come into the house, His disciples asked Him privately, "Why could we not cast it out?"

²⁹So He said to them, "This kind can come out by nothing but prayer and fasting.

This is the fourth and final exorcism in the Gospel of Mark. The disciples were unable to perform the exorcism, so Jesus performed it, emphasizing the necessity of faith.

As believers, it is not enough for us to pray in faith, but we must pray for faith. Faith is trust in God despite the difficulty of the circumstances.

If we are honest with ourselves, we must acknowledge that we don't always have great faith, mountain-moving faith, or even pure faith.

James 2:17 reads, "In the same way, faith by itself, if it is not accompanied by action, is dead."

Hebrews 11:6 reads, "But without faith *it is* impossible to please *Him,* for he who comes to God must believe that He is, and that He is a rewarder of those who diligently seek Him."

Often, our faith is scared and riddled with holes having been dragged through the turmoil and disappointments of life.

God takes special joy in receiving requests for faith. Jesus' strong response in the passage, in verse 22 to this father's questioning of his ability to do anything, causes the man to acknowledge the weakness of his faith and then request more faith. "I believe, help my unbelief."

When our faith is weak it may seem that God is being cold or cruel in not coddling us in our misery. However, it is sometimes God's challenges that ignite our greatest leaps of faith.

So let us believe and let us pray that this same faith by which we pray may not falter. The Lord gives us his Holy Spirit, that we may have the confidence and boldness we need to ask our heavenly Father for his help and grace. Do you trust in God's love and care for you, and pray with expectant faith, that he will give you what you need?

In Matthew 11:22-25, [22]Jesus told his disciples, Have faith in God! [23]If you have faith in God and don't doubt, you can tell this mountain to get up and jump into the sea, and it will. [24]Everything you ask for in prayer will be yours, if you only have faith. [25-26]Whenever you stand up to pray, you must forgive what others have done to you. Then your Father in heaven will forgive your sins.

What kind of faith does the Lord expect of us, especially when we face challenges and difficulties? Ask God to help you strengthen your faith.

May God bless you and keep you is my prayer. Amen.

Notes: _____

_____

_____

_____

_____

_____

_____

_____

_____

_____

_____

_____

_____

God Cannot Be Mocked

Galatians 6:7-10 (NKJV)

[7]Do not be deceived: God cannot be mocked. A man reaps what he sows. [8]Whoever sows to please their flesh, from the flesh will reap destruction; whoever sows to please the Spirit, from the Spirit will reap eternal life. [9]Let us not become weary in doing good, for at the proper time we will reap a harvest if we do not give up. [10]Therefore, as we have opportunity, let us do good to all people, especially to those who belong to the family of believers.

The church has been in existence for many years and will continue to exist for many more. There have always been issues in the church and there will always be issues in the church because we are imperfect human beings and we *are* the church.

The key issues for the church in Galatia were: How do people become acceptable to God? What do people need to do to earn God's favor? How do people become members of God's family? For Paul, the answer was simple: There is nothing we can or need to do. Only Christ could do and has done what must be done to make people acceptable to God. We should simply receive his gift, gratefully thank Him for what he has done for us, and trust Him.

In Verse 7, Paul is saying we cannot mock the justice of God. In other words, we cannot fool God by pretending to be someone we're not. God knows us far better than we know ourselves.

Verse 8 teaches that persons who trust in their friends, themselves, money, or anything else, rather than trust in God, live to satisfy their own sinful nature. Those persons will harvest decay and death. We may not live to see it, but believe me, it will happen. Whoever lives by the Spirit's power and trusts in God will harvest everlasting life (Verse 9).

Over the years I have heard elderly persons say, "I'm tired, I've been working for a long time, let the young people do something. I have put in my time." Wrong! No one is too old to serve God. We must keep growing, maturing, and serving to the end of our days. To idle away our last years is to rob the church of the choicest gifts God has given to share. There is service to be rendered. There is still much to be done. Luke 10:2 says, "…the harvest is plentiful but workers are few…" So pray to the Lord who is in charge of the harvest; ask Him to send more workers. Ephesians 2:10 (NJKV) says, "For we are His workmanship, created in Christ Jesus for good works, which God prepared beforehand that we should walk in them." That lets us know that we must keep running with endurance the race God has set before us, so we not only finish the course, but finish strong. That's how we reap our harvest, by continuing to do good work – not giving up and not quitting.

Finally, verse 10 of Galatians chapter 6 is the bookend of these four verses. "Therefore (to that end) Freedom in the spirit compels us to do good to others in LOVE. Doing good in love to those in the family of faith demonstrates God's faithfulness to his children." Love is the reason we are here today. The Scripture in John 3:16 tells us: "For God so loved the world that He gave His only begotten Son, that whoever believes in Him should not perish but have everlasting life." As we continue our faith walk, "Let us not become weary in doing good, and if we do become weary, don't give up because in the end we will reap a harvest of eternal life" (Galatians 6:9).

May God continue to bless you and keep you is my prayer. Amen.

Notes: _____

_____

_____

_____

_____

_____

The Bible Pattern

The Bible is filled with accounts of God's greatest servants battling to overcome sin. In nearly every case, they had to learn difficult and sometimes painful lessons. When examined collectively, Moses, Noah, David, Samuel, Peter, and others are seen to have fought every kind of problem known to man.

They battled sins, weaknesses, faults, attitudes, and pulls and temptations of the flesh. David fought sins and wrong attitudes and overcame them. Moses lacked faith and confidence and had a temper that he had to overcome. Yet, he will hold a great office in God's kingdom. Both Job and Elijah fought discouragement and depression, even to the point of wanting to die. But these men endured—they overcame. They slew their problems, rather than being slain by them!

These men were actively trained by God and had to overcome Satan, the temptations of this world and the pulls of the flesh. A Christian is one who overcomes his problems, weaknesses, sins, and wrong attitudes, rather than being overcome and defeated by them.

The second verse of Galatians chapter 6 says, "Share each other's burdens, and in this way, obey the law of Christ." A burden is a heaviness of the heart, spirit, or soul—something that weighs us down emotionally, mentally, or spiritually.

Sometimes we feel that sharing our burdens with others is a sign of weakness. Oftentimes, we carry loads the Lord never meant for us to bear alone.

Carrying each other's burdens fulfills the law of Christ to love one another. Galatians 5:13-14 NLT says, [13]"For you have been called to live in freedom, my brothers and sisters. But don't use your freedom to satisfy your sinful nature. Instead, use your freedom to serve one another in love. [14] For the whole law can be summed up in this one command: 'Love your neighbor as yourself.'"

How do we go about bearing each other's loads?

1. Take the appropriate action: Get involved. Getting to know others places us in a position to recognize how to best help them.
2. Have the right purpose in mind: Restoration. We should work to restore the emotional, spiritual, mental, or physical health of others.
3. Have the right motive: Love. John 13:34 tells us, "A new commandment I give to you, that you love one another, even as I have loved you, that you also love one another." 1 Peter 4:8 says, "Above all, keep fervent in your love for one another, because love covers a multitude of sins."
4. Have the right attitude: Gentleness. We must approach others with compassion when bearing their burdens. A gentle person is one who is patient, caring, loving, kind, forgiving, and accepting.

Are you ready and available? The Lord wants you to be the type of person that He could use to restore suffering saints to wholeness. Get ready by putting your own life in order so that you can help others return to fellowship with God.

Those with a proud attitude wrongly assume they are too important to help the weak. Instead of regarding ourselves as better than others, we should examine our own work to ensure that we obey Christ in everything.

If believers carry their own load, they will have no occasion to treat a brother or sister with contempt.

Many times, we worry about what everyone else is doing and complain about what we think others are not doing. Everyone's part is their portion: take care of your portion and leave each person to take care of theirs. God made you to do what you're doing, so do that!

Living by the Spirit results in doing good and reaping rewards from your work. Galatians 6:9-10 tells us, [9]"So let's not get tired of doing what is good. At just the right time we will reap a harvest of blessing if we don't give up. [10] Therefore, whenever we have the opportunity, we should do good to everyone—especially to those in the family of faith."

Paul outlines how to treat other Christians when they sin. Perhaps some of the Galatians were proud of their obedience to the law of their spiritual freedom and willpower. But those who are truly godly are not proud of their accomplishments, but humbly help others.

Be careful: We are all susceptible to the same temptation to sin.

Notes: _____

_____

_____

_____

_____

_____

_____

_____

_____

_____

_____

_____

_____

_____

_____

Count It All Joy

James 1:2-4: (NLT)

[2] Dear brothers and sisters, when troubles of any kind come your way, consider it an opportunity for great joy. [3] For you know that when your faith is tested, your endurance has a chance to grow. [4] So let it grow, for when your endurance is fully developed, you will be perfect and complete, needing nothing.

The bible repeatedly says that God has promised to meet all our needs: "And my God will meet all your needs according to the riches of his glory in Christ Jesus" (Philippians 4:19 [NIV]).

But the Bible also tells us that with every promise there is a condition. Yes, the Lord will give us the desires of our hearts, but first we must delight ourselves in Him. Another condition for this promise is that you have to trust him. The more you trust God, the more God is able to meet needs in your life.

So, how can you learn to trust God more so he can meet all of your needs? How can you learn to have greater faith?

You don't get faith by sitting in a Bible Study group or just talking about it. Faith is like a muscle; it develops by being used. The more you use your faith, the more it gets stretched. And the more it gets stretched, the more God is able to bless your life.

We call the circumstances that God creates to stretch our faith "trials." 1 Peter 1:7 (NLT) says, "These trials will show that your faith is genuine. It is being tested as fire tests and purifies gold."

There are a number of common trials that God uses to test our faith, and, chances are, you're in one of these tests right now. When you go through them, you can know that it is an opportunity for you to develop your faith so you can trust God more.

One test God might use is the *pressure test*. The pressure test asks the question, "How will you handle stress?" Will you depend on yourself, or will you depend on God? Psalm 50:15 says, "Call on me in the day of trouble; I will deliver you, and you will honor me" (NIV). Turn to God when you're in trouble and not to other things.

Another test God might use is the *people test*. God often uses people in your life to test, stretch, and develop your faith. This test asks the question, "How will you handle disappointment?" Life is often disappointing. Careers, marriages, and even plans don't turn out the way we expected. But the most disappointing thing in life is people. Why? We get disappointed by people because we expect them to meet a need that only God himself can meet. This is a test!

Your problem is not the people in your life. Your problem is your response to the people in your life. People are not the problem, and they're not the answer to the problem, either. The answer is God. When you expect a person to be your savior, you're setting yourself up for disappointment.

Jeremiah 17:7 says, "Blessed are those who trust in the Lord and have made the Lord their hope and confidence" (NLT). What happens if you trust in the Lord? Look at God's promise in Isaiah 49:23: "Those who hope in me will not be disappointed" (NIV).

There are several possible attitudes we can take toward tests and trials of life. We can rebel against them by adopting a spirit of defiance, boasting that we will battle through to victory by our own power. On the other hand, we can lose heart or give up under pressure. This is nothing but fatalism. Fatalism is the belief that what will happen has already been decided and cannot be changed. It leads to questioning even the Lord's care for us. Again, we can grumble and complain about our troubles. This is what Paul warned us against in 1 Corinthians 10:10 when he said, "And don't grumble as some of them did, and then were destroyed by the angel of death."

Another option we can indulge in is self-pity: Thinking of no one but ourselves, trying to get sympathy from others. Or better yet, we can be exercised by the difficulties and perplexities of life. We can say in effect, God has allowed this trial to come to me. He has some good purpose in it for me. We may not know what that purpose is, but maybe we should try to find out. We should want God's purposes to work in our lives.

This is what James meant when he said, "My brethren, count it all joy when you fall into various trials." Don't rebel! Don't faint! Rejoice! These problems are not enemies bent on destroying you. They are friends who have come to aid you to develop Christian character.

God is trying to produce Christ-likeness in each of His children. This process necessarily involves suffering, frustration, and perplexity. The fruit of the Spirit cannot be produced when all is sunshine; there must be rain and dark clouds. Trials never seem pleasant; they seem very difficult and disagreeable. But afterward they yield the peaceable fruit of righteousness to those who are trained by them. How many times do we hear a Christian say after passing through some great crisis, "It wasn't easy to take, but I wouldn't give up the experience for anything?"

James speaks of the testing of our faith. He pictures faith as a precious metal, which is being tried by God to see if it is genuine. The metal is subject to the fires of persecution, sickness, suffering, or sorrow. Without problems, we would never develop endurance. Even men of the world realize that problems strengthen character.

James 1:4 says, "But let patience have its perfect work." Sometimes when problems come, we become desperate and use frantic means to cut short the trial, without consulting the Lord as to His purpose in the matter. We should not short circuit the development of endurance in our lives. By cooperating with God, we will become mature, well-rounded Christians, lacking in none of the graces of the Spirit.

We should never become despondent or discouraged when passing through trials. No trial is too great for our Father. Some problems in life are never removed. We must learn to accept them and to prove His grace is sufficient. Paul asked the Lord three times to remove a physical infirmity. The Lord did not remove the infirmity, but He gave Paul grace to bear it.

When we face problems in life that God obviously isn't going to remove, we must be submissive. 2 Chronicles 20:17 says, "But you will not even need to fight. Take your positions; then stand still and watch the Lord's victory..."

We all go through tough times. We go through hardships of every kind. There are times when we feel like giving up. We may become discouraged and not feel like continuing to fight the battles of life.

We may feel like we are on a treadmill running with everything we have and getting nowhere. Life can become stale and boring. Sometimes we may feel as if we can't muster enough energy to continue life's journey.

All of us feel this way at times. No one is exempt from trouble and trials. It happens to the best of people. But we have to keep going even though it may seem as if the challenges and demands of life are going to get the best of us. It is like there is no place to hide when hardships come knocking at our door. No matter how hard we try to keep it out of our lives, somehow it always manages to find its way in.

A gifted hymn-writer wrote these lines as a girl:

"O what a happy soul am I

Although I cannot see;

I am resolved that in this world

Contented I will be.

How many blessings I enjoy

That other people don't,

To weep and sigh because I'm blind

I cannot and I won't."

Just because we have faith and serve the Lord doesn't mean we are free from worry and care.

Peace comes through submission to the will of God. Some problems in life are removed when we have learned our lesson from them. As soon as the Refiner sees His reflection in the molten metal, He turns off the heat.

Most of us lack wisdom to view the pressures of life from God's standpoint. We adopt a short-range view, occupying ourselves with the immediate discomfort. We forget that God's unhurried purpose is to enlarge us through pressure. We read in Isaiah 40:31, *"but they who wait for the LORD shall renew their strength; they shall mount up with wings like eagles..."*

The fact is we don't have to face problems of life in our own wisdom. If, in times of trials, we lack spiritual insight we should go to God and tell Him all about our problems. A songwriter wrote, *"Jesus knows all about our struggles, He will guide till the day is done. There's not a friend like the lowly Jesus, no not one, no not one."*

Those who can trust that God is still sovereign in their darkest struggle and pain shall not go unrewarded. He will give you the power and hope you need to stay in the race and not give up. It was by his grace that you were taken this far, and he will not let you be destroyed now. Surrender your fears and frustrations to God and let him give you his peace to endure.

We need not fear the tests that God brings to us; rather, we need only to trust Him to bring us through them. Why? Because God is good, faithful, and true, knowing that we will end up better than we were before. Once again, God causes all things to work for our good, even if for a short time, it doesn't make sense, it hurts, or it is difficult. We will be the better for it. So, as James so accurately stated, *we can consider it all joy.*

It's not how you get through the storm; it's how you dance in the rain. If it's raining in your life, count it all joy. The sun will come out tomorrow.

God Bless you and keep you is my prayer. Amen.

Notes: _____

_____

_____

_____

_____

_____

_____

_____

_____

_____

_____

_____

_____

_____

_____

_____

_____

_____

_____

_____

_____

_____

Allow the Lord to Shape and Mold You

Jeremiah 18:1-6 (NLT)

¹The LORD gave another message to Jeremiah. He said, ²"Go down to the potter's shop, and I will speak to you there." ³ So I did as he told me and found the potter working at his wheel. ⁴ But the jar he was making did not turn out as he had hoped, so he crushed it into a lump of clay again and started over. ⁵ Then the LORD gave me this message: ⁶ "O Israel, can I not do to you as this potter has done to his clay? As the clay is in the potter's hand, so are you in my hand."

The Lord had Jeremiah take part in an object lesson. What Jeremiah observed at the potter's shop became a picture of what the Lord was about to do with Judah. Jeremiah watched as the potter formed an earthen jar, then crushed it and started over. The Lord likened himself to this potter. He could set standards of perfection and choose to destroy it or reshape his work.

The word of the Lord to Jeremiah is very befitting because it holds within itself a powerful truth principle that we need if we are to grow to increase and favor in our lives.

The prophet in verse one was summoned by the Lord, and in verse two he is told to "Arise…" – this is a very powerful word because, we have to assume that Jeremiah was in a lowered posture while being in the presence of the Lord.

To arise simply denotes the ability to be governed by the Holy Spirit. If we look back over our lives, we will find that the trouble we got ourselves into was a result of not being *ruled* by the spirit of God. If you and I would be totally honest with ourselves, we struggle with being *led* or governed by the Holy Spirit because we have been so used to doing things in our flesh. **This is where we get into the most trouble because God wants to take us in one direction and then the next thing you know, we go into another.**

Today we have too many believers that think themselves to be something when in fact, they are nothing, and carry about themselves a restrictive pride. Jeremiah, known as the weeping prophet, understood that God was to be reverenced.

The Bible clearly states that we are to show reverence to God and to the things that represent His person and presence. The writer of Hebrews wrote, "Let us be thankful, and so worship God acceptably with reverence and awe, for our "God is a consuming fire" (Hebrews. 12:28,29).

The truth be told, salvation is about surrendering your life over to the Christ and allow Christ to take full charge of that life, infusing it with HIS glory and power. Salvation is not merely about going to heaven when you live right; in fact, it encompasses making the invisible God visible so that others might be captivated by the outworking of HIS power in, over and through our life.

The other thing that I love about what Jeremiah is hearing from the Lord is this: After he arises, God tells him, "…go down to the potter's house…" a place that many of us don't want to go, but remember when your life belongs to God, you go where HE directs, pulls, and prods, because it is HE who has made us and not we ourselves.

Psalms 100:3 says, "Know that the LORD, He is God; It is He who has made us, and not we ourselves; We are His people and the sheep of His pasture."

I believe, for the most part, we have endured many times of unnecessary sufferings which could have probably been avoided had we gone down *to the potter's house* when He told us to. Going down to the potter's house is not easy for some, and it is even harder to allow the potter (God) access to your clay (your will, your form).

Jeremiah goes down to the potter's house to observe what he is about to be told. God is not as shallow as we like to portray Him to be. God knows how to speak our language and connect with our understanding before HE engages in changing us. Some Christians can change their clothes three times a day, clean on the outside and filthy on the inside.

Going down to the potter's house is the ability to be positioned in a place of divine instruction and counsel. Never take for granted the things that are around you, because in the place of quietness, the voice of the Lord will speak to our inward parts to bring the change we need. **"Arise, and go down to the potter's house," is the message of salvation and deliverance that must be preached into our spirit, soul, and body to transform us into what God wants us to be in the Kingdom of God.**

Jeremiah is invited to witness how God works in the life of HIS people. Jeremiah is shown the mystery of sanctification and processing through the craftsmanship of the *natural* potter and his wheel. How awesome is that?

God reveals to Jeremiah an intimate look at the love of God in the hand of the potter. He witnesses the stillness of the clay becoming one with the *wheel of change* and transformation as the potter uses the strength of His hands, the force of spinning and watering to soften the clay, and the shaping tools to etch the will of God into the clay. God will spin us through trial and testing, HE will turn us upon the wheel of change, while skillfully applying the right amount of water (The Word), to promote the change needed in the shaping of our clay.

The Scriptures declare that Christ, while walking upon this earth, learned obedience through the things that he suffered. I, too, have learned obedience through the things that I've suffered: some necessary and some not so necessary, but I learned obedience anyway.

The stubbornness of our own flesh many times does not wish to conform to The *Potter* and *HIS* wheel of change. Staying on the wheel makes our change easy to accomplish and with the proper application of Scripture we will become what God will have us to be.

Many times, we rely on the preaching from the pulpit to change us or ministries we are involved in at church, but it is being in the presence of God that will change you. 1 Samuel 10:6 (NIV) says, "The Spirit of the LORD will come powerfully upon you, and you will prophesy with them; and you will be changed into a different person." It is God's intimate touch (the hands working the clay) that will impact our lives more readily and consistently than what we do in church. We have to ask ourselves, "Am I doing something for God, or am I doing something in the power of God?"

In closing, I believe the message here is we are not perfect. There will be times that the manufacturer (God) will have to do a recall because we sometimes become marred or defected and God will remake us into what He wants us to be, if we allow Him.

Going down to the potter's house causes us to hear the Lord's words. Not man, not our denomination, not our logic, but the Word of the Lord.

Will you allow God the opportunity to bring you down to *the potter's house* to invoke change in you, to you and through you?

Know that the LORD, He is God; It is He who has made us, and not we ourselves; We are His people and the sheep of His pasture.

Most gracious Father, You are the One we turn to for help in moments of weakness and times of need. We ask you to be with your servants in whatever illnesses they are suffering. You said in your word in Psalm 107:20 that you send out your Word and heal. So then, please send your healing Word to your servants. In the name of Jesus, drive out all infirmity and sickness from their bodies. Father, I ask you to turn this weakness into strength, suffering into compassion, sorrow into joy, and pain into comfort for others. Father I pray that they trust in your goodness and hope in your faithfulness, even in the middle of this suffering. Let them be filled with patience and joy in your presence as they wait for your healing touch.

Restore your servant to full health, dear Father. Remove all fear and doubt from their hearts by the power of your Holy Spirit, and may you, Lord, be glorified through their lives.

Father, we pray that you will bless persons who are facing trials. Father, we pray that you will remind those persons, "You promised that You would never leave us or forsake us!" It is when we are weak that You are strong. Lord, we pray that you will strengthen their hearts. Be with them in the midst of their trials. Give them the peace that surpasses all understanding. You have promised to keep us in perfect peace when our minds and hearts are fixed upon You, rather than the besetting problems that confront us daily. Help them to wholeheartedly seek You and rely on You surrounding them with Your love.

Jesus was fully God, yet He was fully man. As a man, His power, wisdom, and grace flowed not from His divine nature, but from His utter dependence on God. "The Son can do nothing of Himself," He said (John 5:19). How much did Jesus do apart from God? Nothing.

Jesus always depended on His Father. Luke reports that as news of Jesus' ministry spread, "Great multitudes came together to hear, and to be healed by Him of their infirmities. So He Himself often withdrew into the wilderness and prayed" (Luke 5:15-16). He knew He needed those quiet times to restore His soul.

But you say, "I'm in a place where I can't be useful." Perhaps you feel that circumstances limit you drastically. Illness, financial problems, a difficult boss or co-worker, or an uncooperative family member seem to conspire against you. Whatever your situation, use it to grow closer to the Savior. God can use anyone.

Mentor: The word *mentor* soon came to mean "a wise and responsible tutor"—an experienced person who advises, guides, teaches, inspires, challenges, corrects, and serves as a model.

Second Timothy 2:2 describes spiritual mentoring, and the Bible gives us many examples. Timothy had Paul; Mark had Barnabas; Joshua had Moses; Elisha had Elijah.

But what about today? Who will love and work with new Christians and help them grow spiritually strong? Who will encourage, guide, and model the truth for them? Who will call young believers to accountability and work with God to help mold their character?

Will you become one whom God can use to impart wisdom and to help others grow toward maturity? God teaches us so that we can teach others.

A good man is hard to find these days. At least that's the impression you might get from a society that is having a tough time finding heroes.

Too often, though, we look in the wrong places when we're searching for role models. We look for someone who is a good athlete or who makes a lot of money or who commands respect because of leadership skills.

When we look only in these situations for good men, we fail to see that most of the godly men are not in the spotlight. They are just quietly and faithfully serving their families, their friends, and God.

In Psalm 112 we see a clear set of guidelines for what makes a man good. According to the psalmist, a good man fears the Lord (v.1), delights in God's commands (v.1), and is gracious, compassionate, and righteous (v.4). He is generous and exercises discretion (v.5). He is unshakable in his faith, and he has no fear because his trust is in God (vs.6-8).

Looking for a good man? In a society where so many are anything but godly, how can we set the right example? Look at Psalm 112. It's a pattern all Christian men (and women) need to follow if they want to make a difference in their world. — Dave Branon

> The model of a man is he
> Whose life is strong and true,
> Who loves the Lord with all his heart
> And seeks His will to do. —DJD

To make a difference in the world, let Jesus make a difference in you.

Notes: _____

_____

_____

_____

The Word Became Flesh

John 1:1-3 (NKJV)

In the beginning was the Word, and the Word was with God, and the Word was God. ² He was in the beginning with God. ³ All things were made through Him, and without Him nothing was made that was made.

I am going to share a few sentences from the daily devotion from January 6, 2015.

The title for that devotion was, "The Word Became Flesh and Dwelt Among Us."

The Word became flesh and blood and moved into the neighborhood. We saw the glory with our own eyes, the one-of-a-kind glory, like Father, like Son: generous inside and out, true from start to finish. Jesus was a living Bible. John 1:1 tells us, "...the Word was God...," so the more you get into the Word and it gets into you, the more of God you're depositing within you. Another part of that devotion reads, "A word to the wise: When you start studying the Bible, don't do it to find some new truth nobody else has ever seen. Do it with the attitude, 'Lord, what are you saying to me?'"

John raises the curtain of his Gospel with a stunning description of Jesus Christ as "the Word" (the divine wisdom manifest in the creation, government, and redemption of the world and often identified with the second person of the Trinity). Both Greek and Jewish listeners in the first century would immediately recognize the profound meaning of this title. Greeks would have of seminal forces (having a strong influence on ideas, works, events) that sustain the universe. Jewish minds would have thought back to God creating the world with his word. John anchors the divinity of Jesus in this ancient Jewish concept of Wisdom. The divine Wisdom that had existed from before time with God can now be known in Jesus Christ.

The problem most of us have isn't interpreting the difficult passages; it's obeying the ones we already understand. The Word provides two things: protection and direction. Psalm 119:92-93 (NLT) explains protection: "If your instructions hadn't sustained me with joy, I would have died in my misery. [93] I will never forget your commandments, for by them you give me life."

Psalm 99:105 explains direction: "Your word is a lamp to my feet, And a light to my path." Please know that the path you take determines your destination; so before you decide to go in a certain direction, talk to God. Don't be surprised when he takes you down a road you have not known. Just trust that God knows what He's doing.

The simple reason why the Son of God is called the Word seems to be that as our words explain our minds to others, so was the Son of God sent in order to reveal his Father's mind to the world. What the evangelist says of Christ proves that he is God. He asserts His existence in the beginning; His coexistence with the Father. The Word was with God. In the beginning, Genesis 1:1 starts with the moment of creation and moves forward to the creation of humanity. John 1:1 starts with creation and contemplates eternity. The fact that the word was with God, suggests a face-to-face relationship in the ancient world was important. That people of equal status be on the same level, or face- to-face when sitting across from one another was important. Thus, the word, which indicates a personal relationship also implies equal status. The word Jesus Christ, Himself, is an active person in communication with the father. Look at 1 John 1:2, Moreover, the Word was God. The word order in Greek shows that the word was God, not a god. This is a straightforward declaration of Christ's deity since John uses word to refer to Jesus. The word was of the very quality of God while still retaining His personal distinction from the Father.

All things were made by him, and not as an instrument. Without him, was not anything made that was made, from the highest angel to the meanest worm? This shows how well qualified he was for the work of our redemption and salvation. Let us pray without ceasing, that our eyes may be opened to behold this Light, that we may walk in it and be made wise unto salvation, by faith in Jesus Christ.

The Word is who God is. It's His thoughts. It's His testimony. It's His declaration to man everything He has in store, what He has done and will do. It's His wisdom, His power, His mercy, His grace and truth. The Word is the Spirit of Truth manifested in the flesh. It is God's ONLY begotten Son, Jesus Christ. Without God's Word, Jesus, nothing would be in existence. Jesus is not God. He is the Son of the true and living God. We must have God's Word abiding in our hearts in order to know how to live, how to walk, and that we have the Spirit of Truth and not the Spirit of Error. It is the Holy Ghost that witnesses and testifies of who Jesus is. God Himself testified of His Son, when He spoke out of heaven and declared, "This is my beloved Son, in whom I am well pleased, hear him." These are the above mentioned: the Father, the Word Jesus, and the Holy Ghost. Nothing that was made was made without the Word, which became flesh. Jesus is the Word spoken by God. John 1:17 says, "For the law was given by Moses, but grace and truth came by Jesus Christ." He is God's Word that gives light to all who are in darkness. 1John 1:1-2 says, "That which was from the beginning, which we have heard, which we have seen with our eyes, which we have looked upon, and our hands have handled, of the Word of Life. For the life was manifested, and we have seen it, and bear witness and shew you that eternal life, which was with the Father and was manifested unto us."

In the beginning was the Word, and the Word was with God, and the Word was God. May God continue to bless and keep you close to Him, is my prayer. Amen.

Notes: _____

_____

_____

_____

_____

Jesus Walks on Water

Matthew 14:23-33 (NJKV)

[23]And when He had sent the multitudes away, He went up on the mountain by Himself to pray. Now when evening came, He was alone there. [24]But the boat was now in the middle of the sea, [a] tossed by the waves, for the wind was contrary.[25]Now in the fourth watch of the night Jesus went to them, walking on the sea. [26] And when the disciples saw Him walking on the sea, they were troubled, saying, "It is a ghost!" And they cried out for fear.[27]But immediately Jesus spoke to them, saying, "Be of good cheer! It is I; do not be afraid." [28]And Peter answered Him and said, "Lord, if it is you, command me to come to you on the water." [29]So He said, "Come." And when Peter had come down out of the boat, he walked on the water to go to Jesus. [30]But when he saw that the wind *was* boisterous,[b] he was afraid; and beginning to sink he cried out, saying, "Lord, save me!" [31]And immediately Jesus stretched out *His* hand and caught him, and said to him, "O you of little faith, why did you doubt?" [32]And when they got into the boat, the wind ceased. [33]Then those who were in the boat came and [c] worshiped Him, saying, "Truly You are the Son of God."

Jesus walking on water is one of his miracles in the New Testament. There are three accounts in the Gospels: Matthew 14:22–33, Mark 6:45–52 and John 6:16–21. This story follows the miracle of the feeding of the five thousand.

Most of us have heard this text preached many times, but if you would, imagine yourself in Peter's shoes.

Think about it: you are four miles out in the middle of Tiberias Sea (On the Sea of Galilee). The time is between 3 and 6 in the morning. You're rowing with all your strength because you're under the instruction of Jesus to go to the other side. But there's a storm, and the winds are blowing, and the waves are violently beating against the boat. You are experiencing a situation where you are literally out of control. It's dark, and the mist from the sea obscures your vision. You look out over the waters, and it looks like there's someone walking on water.

If I were on that boat, I would have thought it was a ghost as the other disciples did. The reason they thought it may have been a ghost is, back then, there was a cultural superstition that the souls of persons who died in the seas roamed the water.

So here is Peter, in the midst of that situation. The mist begins to clear, he sees that it's Jesus.

He cries out: "Lord, if it's you, bid me come to you on the water." [29]So He said, "Come." And when Peter had come down out of the boat, he walked on the water to go to Jesus.

So, Peter gets out of the boat and start walking toward Jesus. Peter's intentions were, "I've got to get to Jesus."

Saints of God, we must be intent on getting to Jesus. If we look at Peter in this situation, we see his intentions were good. And yes, I have heard that the road to hell is paved with good intentions. But when your good intentions are coupled with the word of God, then your intentions become a manifestation of the revelation. When the good that you would do is coupled in faith with the word of God, it is the word of God that gives you the power to do good that you ordinarily would not do.

Peter is walking on water, but when Peter shifts his focus, he begins to sink. If the truth be told, we all sink. Anyone that's human will experience a sinking reality. While Peter is sinking, Jesus is still standing there in the middle of the sea. Jesus wants to be as close as you allow him. When Peter started sinking, all Jesus did was reach out and grab him because he was just that close. The problem is when you start to sink, the Lord is a great distance away from you. That's why we always have to stay close to the Lord.

The Lord wants to be close with us. Every time we pray that means He's coming closer. Every time we request of Him, that means He's coming closer.

I realize Christians go to church for different reasons, but we must go to church to worship and praise God. In order to worship and praise God, we must be prepared to worship and praise God. When we come to church and think about the goodness of Jesus and all He brought us through, we can't help but to worship and praise Him. Lord, thank you, because I would have drowned if you hadn't reached out your hand and grabbed me. Lord, thank you, because I should have been dead. Lord, thank you that I didn't turn out like that. Lord, thank you, because you healed my body. Lord, thank you, because you woke me up this morning. Lord, thank you, because you gave me another chance. Lord, thank you, because it could have gone the other way. Lord, I thank you.

I believe this miracle of Jesus and Peter walking on water was intended to show the importance of faith, and the control of Jesus over nature.

In closing, God challenges us sometimes and allow the winds to howl and the waves to roar, but you've got to keep walking in faith toward Jesus. That's the test we all have to go through, to make sure that our faith is valid. Though storms keep raging in my life (and sometimes it's hard to tell night from day), still the hope that lies within is reassured. As I keep my eyes upon the distant shore, I know He'll lead me safely to that blessed place He has prepared. But, if the storm doesn't cease and if the winds keep blowing in my life, my soul has been anchored in the Lord.

May God continue to bless you and keep you is my prayer. Amen.

Notes: _____

_____

_____

_____

_____

Rejoice Always

Psalm 100:1-5 (KJV)

[1]Make a joyful noise unto the Lord, all ye lands. [2]Serve the Lord with gladness: come before his presence with singing. [3]Know ye that the Lord he is God: it is he that hath made us, and not we ourselves; we are his people, and the sheep of his pasture. [4]Enter into his gates with thanksgiving, and into his courts with praise: be thankful unto him, and bless his name. [5]For the Lord is good; his mercy is everlasting; and his truth endureth to all generations.

I learned Psalms 1, 23, and 100 in second grade when we were allowed to pray and read Scriptures in school.

Psalm 100 is a Psalm of thanksgiving. This Psalm calls all nations to come to Jerusalem to worship the Lord and to acknowledge his goodness to Israel.

Make a joyful noise unto the LORD: Making a joyful noise to the Lord means that we acknowledge that God should be worshipped by a cheerful people; and a cheerful spirit is in keeping with God's nature, his acts, and the gratitude, which we should cherish for his mercies. A songwriter wrote: *"Great is thy faithfulness, morning-by-morning new mercies I see."*

Serve the LORD with gladness: He is our Lord, and therefore he is to be served; come before his presence with singing. Another songwriter wrote: *"Let those refuse to sing Who never knew our God; But favorites of the heavenly king must speak his praise abroad."*

Know ye that the Lord, he is God: We ought to know whom we worship and why.

Enter into his gates with thanksgiving: Back then the Gate Courts were a part of the Temple. Mercy permits us to enter his gates; let us praise that mercy.

For the Lord is good: This sums up his character and contains a mass of reasons for praise. He is good, gracious, kind, bountiful, loving;

yes, God is love. And he who does not praise the good is not good himself.

Notes: _____

_____

_____

_____

_____

_____

_____

_____

_____

_____

_____

_____

_____

_____

_____

_____

_____

_____

_____

_____

God Has Everything You Need

1 Thessalonians 5:16-18 (NKJV)

[16] Rejoice always, [17] pray without ceasing, [18] in everything give thanks; for this is the will of God in Christ Jesus for you.

I chose this passage of Scripture because there is always something going on. Just look at the news. Even in our lives we will have those ups and downs. Paul reminds us to rejoice, always. Be Happy. Then he says to pray without ceasing. We should never stop praying. Never stop praying means not giving up. And then he says, in everything give thanks; for this is the will of God in Christ Jesus for you. Being thankful means you recognize that God is sovereign and can redeem any situation. If we are going to pray without ceasing, we must have faith in God for what we are praying for, so that God may grant our request.

Is your faith out of shape or is it maintaining a healthy diet of prayer?

I learned as a little boy that some toys need batteries to function. Just as batteries power toys, faith powers believers. Biblical knowledge cannot power it, church attendance cannot power it, even being a good person cannot replace the primary function of faith: establishing and developing our relationship with God. In fact, without faith we can have no relationship with God.

We are saved by our faith in the finished work of Jesus on the cross. Faith is the means by which we hold that God exist, and that He rewards those who diligently seek Him. Therefore, when we pray in faith, we are assured of God's reward, which is his presence. We must remember that we are sometimes like batteries. Just like batteries run down, so do we. This is how faith and prayer work together. As we pray, we are recharged. If we have faith we are inspired to pray and lay claim to God's promises. We must recognize that prayer increases faith and faith empowers our prayer life. Therefore, when we pray, we should rise from our knees expecting to see something different than what we saw before we kneeled. Our prayer life must be rooted in faith and we must see prayer as a means by which to reach God and

69

to see God move in our lives. Prayer cannot be something done out of duty, out of obligation or religious routine. Prayer must be viewed as effective by the one who is praying. We have all heard it before: much prayer much power, little prayer little power, no prayer no power.

Is your faith out of shape, or is it maintaining a healthy diet of prayer?

Notes: _____

_____

_____

_____

_____

_____

_____

_____

_____

_____

_____

_____

_____

_____

_____

_____

Safety of Abiding in the Presence of God

Psalm 91:1-7 (NKJV)

[1]He who dwells in the secret place of the Most High Shall abide under the shadow of the Almighty. [2]I will say of the Lᴏʀᴅ, "He is my refuge and my fortress: My God, in Him I will trust." [3]Surely He shall deliver you from the snare of the fowler[a] And from the perilous pestilence. [4]He shall cover you with His feathers, and under His wings you shall take refuge; His truth shall be your shield and buckler. [5]You shall not be afraid of the terror by night, nor of the arrow that flies by day, [6]Nor of the pestilence that walks in darkness, nor of the destruction that lays waste at noonday. [7]A thousand may fall at your side, and ten thousand at your right hand; but it shall not come near you.

This Psalm expresses confidence in the Almighty God, who provides a shelter for those who take refuge in him. They receive redemption, life, and glory from the Lord, who loves and cares for those who seek him. The Most High is an ancient title that expresses the Lord's exalted status as ruler and protector of the godly. He that dwells in the secret place of the Most High. The blessings here promised are not for all believers, but for those who live in close fellowship with God. Every child of God looks toward the inner sanctuary and the mercy seat, yet all do not dwell in the most holy place; they run to it at times, and enjoy occasional approaches, but they do not habitually reside in the mysterious presence. Those who through rich grace obtain unusual and continuous communion with God, so as to abide in Christ and Christ in them, become possessors of rare and special benefits, which are missed by those who follow from a distance, and grieve the Holy Spirit of God.

What Does It Mean to Abide in Christ?

In order for the Father to conform us to the image of His Son (Romans 8:29), "For whom He foreknew, He also predestined *to be* conformed to the image of His Son, that He might be the firstborn among many

71

brethren" we must **abide in Christ**." What does it mean to abide? It means to remain, rest, stay, wait, and continue. Abiding in Christ, then, involves waiting upon the Lord and entering into His peace. "But they that wait upon the LORD shall renew their strength; they shall mount up with wings as eagles; they shall run, and not be weary; and they shall walk, and not faint" (Isaiah 40:31).

[5]"Jesus said, I am the vine, you *are* the branches. He who abides in Me, and I in him, bears much fruit; for without Me you can do nothing" (John 15:5). Just as a branch draws its life-source from the vine, believers must stay connected to Christ for His life to flow through them and produce spiritual fruit. Branches "live and move and have their being" only by the life of the vine.

Abiding in Christ is a patient expectancy; it is neither wasteful idleness nor anxious striving. Psalm 62:5 says, "My soul, wait silently for God alone, for my expectation *is* from Him."

Abiding in Christ, therefore, means to draw supernatural strength from the presence of the Lord and walk moment by moment in the leading of His Spirit.

Abiding in Christ means:

- Bearing spiritual fruit

- Hearing the Word and keeping it in your heart

- Loving Jesus and doing what He says

- Loving others

- Trusting God and making Him your refuge

- Hating the world's system, 1 John 2:15 says, "Do not love the world or the things in the world." If anyone loves the world, the love of the Father is not in him.

- Remaining steadfast in the faith of the Gospel.

The Fruit of Abiding

God looks for the evidence of our abiding in Christ, which is **good fruit**. "But the fruit of the Spirit is love, joy, peace, longsuffering, gentleness, goodness, faith, meekness, temperance" (Galatians 5: 22-23).

The **fruit of the Spirit** comes only out of an abiding relationship with Jesus. It is not brought about by our own strength, nor by the works of the flesh, but only by abiding in Christ (see Matthew 7:19-20).

Jesus said to His disciples, in John 15:7, "If you abide in Me, and My words abide in you, you will[b] ask what you desire, and it shall be done for you." When we abide in Christ and His words abide in us, we bear the fruit of the Spirit and the Father is glorified. This, in fact, is our divine calling.

Those who bear fruit will encounter seasons of **purging** (which means pruning *or* cleansing) in their lives. Jesus said, "Every branch that beareth fruit, he purgeth it, that it may bring forth more fruit" (John 15:2).

The fruit of abiding in Christ will become apparent in your life: Do you love your brother? Do you also love your enemy? Do you enjoy spending time with Jesus in the quiet place and searching out His Word for hidden treasures? Do you have inner peace and joy in chaotic circumstances? These are all evidence of abiding in Christ.

The Tragedy of Not Abiding

Those who do not abide in Christ will be ashamed before Him when He appears. 1 John 2:28 says: "And now, little children, abide in Him, that when He appears, we may have confidence and not be ashamed before Him at His coming." Truly, abiding in Christ is the only way to not be ashamed before Him at His coming. "Then you will know that I *am* the LORD, For they shall not be ashamed who wait for Me." (Isaiah 49:23)

May the Lord bless you and keep you is my prayer. Amen.

Notes: _____

_____

_____

_____

_____

_____

_____

_____

_____

_____

_____

_____

_____

_____

_____

_____

_____

_____

_____

_____

_____

Delight Yourself in the Lord

Psalm 37:4-5 (NKJV)

[4]Delight yourself also in the LORD; And He shall give you the desires of your heart. [5]Commit your way to the LORD; Trust also in Him, And He shall bring it to pass.

Our hearts are always full of desires. Whether it's desire for God, food, friends, money, house, or car – at every waking moment we are always desiring something, which is why the promise of Psalm 37:4 captures our attention: "Delight yourself in the LORD, and he will give you the desires of your heart."

But what does this Scripture mean? I think it's safe to say that if you were to ask 10 different people you would probably get 10 different answers.

I thought this Scripture meant something totally different until I really got into the study. Thank God for the Holy Spirit.

I like to fish. I go fishing early in the morning so I get the opportunity to see the sunrise. So, if I delight myself in the sunrise, while I'm delighting in the sunrise, I'm not desiring anything else.

As I delight in the sunrise, what I desire at that moment is *that sunrise.* I want to keep enjoying the beauty of the sunrise. Later, I might have other desires, but at that moment the sunrise is what I desire.

In the same way, when I delight in the Lord what I desire is *the Lord* — to keep beholding his glory, worshiping his majesty, seeing his beauty.

Take Job, for example. Surely Job desired that God would immediately heal the boils on his body. But God did not give Job this desire of his heart. "And he took for himself a potsherd (a pottery fragment) with which to scrape himself while he sat in the midst of the ashes" (Job 2:8).

Think also of David. David delighted in the Lord and his desire was to build a temple to the Lord. But God did not give David this desire of his heart. [3]"But it happened that night that the word of God came to Nathan, saying, [4]"Go and tell My servant David, 'Thus says the LORD: You shall not build Me a house to dwell in'" (1 Chronicles 17:3-4).

Or take Paul, who also delighted in the Lord, and desired that God remove his thorn in the flesh. But God did not give Paul this desire of his heart. "And He said to me, 'My grace is sufficient for you, for My strength is made perfect in weakness. Therefore, most gladly I will rather boast in my infirmities, that the power of Christ may rest upon me. [10] Therefore I take pleasure in infirmities, in reproaches, in needs, in persecutions, in distresses, for Christ's sake. For when I am weak, then I am strong (2 Corinthians 12: 9-10).

Psalm 37:4 says: "Delight yourself also in the LORD, And He shall give you the desires of your heart." I think this verse means if we truly find satisfaction and worth in Christ, He will give us the longings of our hearts. Does that mean, if we go to church every Sunday, God will give us what we want? Of course not. I believe the idea behind this verse and others like it is that, when we truly rejoice or "delight" in the eternal things of God, our desires will begin to parallel His desires and we will never go unfulfilled. Matthew 6:33 says, "But seek first his kingdom and his righteousness, and all these things [the necessities of life] will be given to you as well."

Many delight in wealth, status, material possessions, and other temporary things of this world, but they are never satisfied.

If we place our joy and hope in God first, He will meet all our needs. He will even grant our wants, as our hearts' desires begin to match up with His will.

Rather than trust our hearts, we are to commit our hearts to God: "Trust in the Lord with all your heart and lean not on your own understanding; in all your ways submit to him, and he will make your paths straight" (Proverbs 3:5-6 NIV). This passage gives an explicit command not to trust ourselves, and it also gives the promise of guidance to those who choose to follow the Lord.

To take delight in the Lord means aligning with the Lord's way in order to enjoy Him.

You can "D-E-L-I-G-H-T yourself in the Lord" when you realize that doing good is always the right choice.

God's love is amazing and never fails. Your eternal life is a guarantee that is sealed on the day you believe in what Jesus went to the cross to do for you. In good times and in bad you can count on the fact that God is our strength, a very present help in times of trouble.

He won't let you fall, and you can trust Him to deliver upon every promise that He ever makes because God is not a man, that he should lie (Numbers 23:19a). Delighting in the Lord is an attitude that says, "I am God's child and He's got my back."

In closing, these few verses are full of promises. God promises to give us a place to live with the physical nourishment of food. Consider this: That dwelling place is more than our Lord Jesus had during His earthly ministry. He spoke of this in Matthew 8:20 when He said, "...The foxes have holes, and the birds of the air have nests; but the Son of man hath not where to lay his head."

We are also promised to obtain the desires of our heart, but that comes with conditions. We are encouraged to delight in the LORD as one condition. Another condition is to "Commit your way to the LORD, Trust also in Him, And He shall bring it to pass" (Psalm 37:5). A command and a promise, how delightful!

May God continue to bless you and keep you is my prayer. Amen.

Notes: _____

The Good News

Colossians1: 3-14 (NKJV)

[3]We give thanks to the God and Father of our Lord Jesus Christ, praying always for you, [4]since we heard of your faith in Christ Jesus and of your love for all the saints; [5]because of the hope which is laid up for you in heaven, of which you heard before in the word of the truth of the gospel, [6]which has come to you, as *it has* also in all the world, and is bringing forth fruit,[b] as *it is* also among you since the day you heard and knew the grace of God in truth; [7]as you also learned from Epaphras, our dear fellow servant, who is a faithful minister of Christ on your behalf, [8]who also declared to us your love in the Spirit.

[9]"For this reason we also, since the day we heard it, do not cease to pray for you, and to ask that you may be filled with the knowledge of His will in all wisdom and spiritual understanding; [10]that you may walk worthy of the Lord, fully pleasing *Him,* being fruitful in every good work and increasing in the knowledge of God; [11]strengthened with all might, according to His glorious power, for all patience and longsuffering with joy; [12]giving thanks to the Father who has qualified us to be partakers of the inheritance of the saints in the light. [13]He has delivered us from the power of darkness and conveyed *us* into the kingdom of the Son of His love, [14]in whom we have redemption through His blood, the forgiveness of sins."

Paul's letter to the Colossians, chapter 1 verse 3, begins with thanksgiving and prayer. [3]"We give thanks to the God and Father of our Lord Jesus Christ, praying always for you." Paul prays that God would grant his readers a deeper understanding of the good news and its full expression in their lives.

The Good News is effective in changing lives and bringing about spiritual growth.

Spiritual Growth yields a cleaner and deeper comprehension of Christian truth and conduct that pleases the Lord, through which a believer will have the endurance and patience to stand firm against evil.

I believe we should be prepared when we go to God in prayer. When we pray, we have an even greater opportunity because prayer gives us a private audience with the King of Kings and Lord of Lords.

Paul begins his letter to the believers in Colossae by telling them that he prays for them always and every day. He prays for them name by name and he prays for them by need. Likewise, we stand in the gap and pray for others as well as we pray for ourselves.

We are taking the time to call up heaven, where angels wait to be dispatched to assist us and to dispense strength to undergird the cause of our hearts, only for us to wallow, meander, and drift from one thing to another without ever expressing a clear request or presenting a clear issue before the throne. Our time in prayer is more fruitful when we are focused.

The Holy Spirit will reveal to you the things He would like to discuss with you. Then once you pray, and your mind begins to wander, as all of ours do, you are able to re-center yourself, get back on track, and make the most of the greatest audience that one can ever encounter – GOD!

What you will discover is that over time, your prayer list will become the record of your testimony. You will find that as you make praying a daily habit, many things on your list will be resolved, yet not all in the manner that you requested. However, you will begin to notice that as you've prayed about a particular issue, you will be in a better position to celebrate your victories, or to heal from your disappointments.

God is a good God. He is a great God; He can do anything but fail. Amen.

Notes: _____

_____

_____

_____

_____

_____

_____

_____

_____

_____

_____

_____

_____

_____

_____

_____

_____

_____

_____

_____

_____

The Armor of God

Ephesians 6:10-18 (NIV)

[10]Finally, be strong in the Lord and in his mighty power. [11]Put on the full armor of God, so that you can take your stand against the devil's schemes. [12]For our struggle is not against flesh and blood, but against the rulers, against the authorities, against the powers of this dark world and against the spiritual forces of evil in the heavenly realms. [13]Therefore put on the full armor of God, so that when the day of evil comes, you may be able to stand your ground, and after you have done everything, to stand. [14]Stand firm then, with the belt of truth buckled around your waist, with the breastplate of righteousness in place, [15]and with your feet fitted with the readiness that comes from the gospel of peace. [16]In addition to all this, take up the shield of faith, with which you can extinguish all the flaming arrows of the evil one. [17]Take the helmet of salvation and the sword of the Spirit, which is the word of God. [18]And pray in the Spirit on all occasions with all kinds of prayers and requests. With this in mind, be alert and always keep on praying for all the Lord's people.

Arm Yourself

Every Christian needs to know how to battle evil. God gives us detailed instructions on how to battle evil.

I appreciate Bible statements promising ability to stand against the Devil. Notice! In verse 11 it says, "Put on the full armor of God." It doesn't say that God will put the armor on us, but that we are to put it on. Nor does it say we are to put on our best willpower, determination, or education. Since man is made a little lower than the angels (and the devil is a fallen angel), our best human tactics are no match against the devil. We can't overcome on our own, neither will God do it without our involvement. Only we can apply to our lives that which only Jesus could have provided for us. In order to stand against any strong temptation to do wrong, we must cover our humanness with God's armor promises of the Bible.

God's armor brings victory because it is far more than a protective covering. It is the very life of Jesus Christ Himself. God has given us the armor and it is up to us to use it. So let's talk about the pieces of armor and their function.

The Belt (of Truth): Ephesians 6:14 reads, "Stand firm in the belt of truth buckled around your waist." The belt of truth involves two places: our hearts and our minds. Truth keeps us secure in Christ and makes effective all the other pieces of armor. The belt of truth holds our armor in place. Commit yourself daily to walk in the light of God's truth. Psalm 86:11 reads, "Teach me your ways, O Lord, that I may live according to your truth!"

The Breastplate (of Righteousness): Ephesians 6:14 reads, "With the breastplate of righteousness in place." A soldier with a breastplate goes into battle boldly with confidence. The devil is constantly attacking with lies, accusations and reminders of past sin. Without the breastplate of righteousness, these will penetrate your heart. Become aware of who you are in Christ Jesus. "Come boldly into His presence" (Hebrews 4:16).

The Shoes (of Peace & Preparation): Ephesians 6:15 reads, "For shoes, put on the peace that comes from the Good News so that you will be fully prepared." Shoes allow us to step freely and without fear while we turn our full attention to the battle at hand. They aid in our movement and defense. The shoes God gives propel us onward to proclaim the true peace, which is available in Christ. Prepare yourself to follow the Lord no matter what.

The Shield (of Faith): Ephesians 6:16 reads, "Above all, taking the shield of faith with which you will be able to quench all the fiery darts of the wicked one." The shield not only defends our whole body but also our armor. The shield of faith has a very specific function, which the Bible makes abundantly clear: quench all the fiery darts of the wicked. Not some, but all of them. The shield moves with the attack, no matter the direction.

The Helmet (of Salvation): Ephesians 6:17 reads, "Take the helmet of salvation…" Satan's target is your mind. Satan's weapon is lies. The enemy wants to make us doubt God and our salvation. The helmet protects our minds from doubting the truth of God's saving work for us. 1 Thessalonians 5:8 reads, "Since we belong to the day, we must be serious and put the armor of faith and love on our chests, and put on a Helmet of the Hope of Salvation."

The Sword (of the Spirit): Ephesians 6:17 reads, Put on "the sword of the Spirit, which is the word of God." The sword of the Spirit is the only weapon of offense in the armor, but the Word/Bible is also a tool for defense. Strongholds, arguments, and thoughts are all weapons the enemy uses against us. With the Sword of the Spirit, God's word, the people are equipped to deal with them all. We need to trust in the truth of God's Word. Have confidence in the value of God's word. Get a hunger and desire for it.

Prayer Ephesians 6:18 reads, "Pray in the Spirit at all times and on every occasion. Stay alert and be persistent in your prayers for all believers everywhere."

In order to put on the "full armor" and enjoy a daily and eternal love-relationship with Jesus Christ, thank Him for what He has shown you in His Word. Know the Scriptures behind your prayer so that your words and faith are grounded in the authority of the Bible.

When the hell hounds are on your back and the devil just won't leave you alone, put on the full armor of God and give thanks!

Notes: _____

_____

_____

_____

_____

Be Still

Psalm 46:10 (NKJV)

"Be still, and know that I *am* God; I will be exalted among the nations, I will be exalted in the earth!"

The definition of still is not moving or without motion, quiet, silent, calm, tranquil, or peaceful.

The command "Be still" is not given to restrict the mobility of God's people. The duty represents a spiritual disposition that ought to characterize those to whom God's unfailing promises have been given.

This command "Be still" forces us to think on two things: that we are finite, and that God is infinite. That being the case, we need to drop our hands, go limp, relax, and "chill out." Christian people ought to "come, behold the works of God, that we may enjoy a calm confidence in him who gave us his Son."

When we face difficulties in our life that would make it seem as if we are on a ship being tossed upon a stormy sea, how exactly can we be still, as well as strength to our family, while a storm rages around us?

I'm sure you've heard the song "My Soul Has Been Anchored in the Lord." The second verse says, *"I realize that sometimes, in this life, we're going to be tossed by the waves and the currents that seem so fierce, but in the Word of God I've got an anchor, and keeps me steadfast, unmovable, despite the tide but if the storm doesn't cease and if the winds keep on blowing in my life, my soul has been anchored in the Lord."*

When we are free from outside noise, we are able to hear the still, small voice of God's Spirit, as he comes to comfort and guide us through our trials. Some of the noise we experience that could be blocking our ability to feel God's presence is our own worry.

When we learn to change our thoughts from negative to positive, we are able to feel God's love because we are in harmony with him. The noise is replaced by a sweet melody of peace.

To be calm does not mean that the storm is no longer all around you, it means that the storm is no longer within you. The storms may still rage, but you are free from the effects of them.

Often, when trials come, we tend to get angry with God and cry out in complaint. When we do this, we lessen our ability to feel the Spirit, because we leave no room in our hearts for the Spirit to dwell. God cannot dwell in a heart that is full of anger. It is when we learn to put at rest our complaints and cast our burdens on the Lord, to hush our cries and wait upon him, that we will find comfort.

Sometimes when difficulties arise, we allow the anger and frustrations from those trials to push us into violence, or we try to force our will upon the Lord. Neither one of these choices will bring us peace. You've heard the song, *"When peace like a river attendeth my way, when sorrows, like sea billows, roll; whatever my lot, thou hast taught me to say, it is well, it is well with my soul."* When conflicts come and we are untroubled by them because of our faith in God, only then can we know peace.

We can learn to be still as we pray, read Scripture, go for a walk, meditate, or give ourselves time to ponder, free from interruption or disturbance. I have the bible on my iPhone and sometimes instead of listening to music while I'm walking, I listen to the bible. This not only allows me to communicate with our Heavenly Father, but it also allows my Heavenly Father to communicate with me.

Often, the busyness of life makes it impossible for us to truly hear what God is trying to tell us. It is when we slow down and allow ourselves the opportunity to rest, that our mind and heart can focus on those things that are of the greatest importance. God wants to talk to us, but we have to be ready and willing to listen.

I learned that the sun does not rise and the sun does not set. It is an illusion. Instead, the sun stays still, steady, and bright, and as the Earth turns to face the sun, that is when the morning comes. The darkness of night comes when the Earth turns away. It is the same with us. In our trials, when we turn to face the Son, who is steady and bright just like the Sun, we are filled with light. If, instead, we choose to turn away from him, the darkness of night will surely come. Choose to face the light.

When we are gentle and easygoing, we are able to hear God's commands. He gently persuades us to love him and serve others. We are able to ease our own troubles, and we will carry God's spirit within us, which will aid us in easing the burdens of others.

When we approach life and our trials in a calm manner, we are able to see the bigger picture and outline a plan of recovery. Not only does it allow us to have a clear mind, it allows us to help calm the fears of those around us.

When our mind and spirit are still, our whole body is at peace. We are able to see things with a clear mind, feel things with a pure heart, and hear the voice of our Heavenly Father with ears that are open and in tune with his spirit. We will know God because we will be one with him.

Sadly, there are those who are far from "still." They "do all the work" and give God none of the credit. They believe that by lifting their hands and by taking credit, they can survive and thrive by the sweat of their own brow. They can do it all on their own, without any divine dependence.

If you are the last man or woman standing, be still. "God is our refuge and strength, a very present help in trouble. Therefore, we will not fear, though the earth does change" (Psalm 46:1-2a). Hallelujah!

"Be still and know that I am God," is not just a saying, it is a state of being. It is the ability to know God well enough to trust in his abilities to rescue you. As we learn to be still and trust in God, we come to know and understand that we are God's children. We are never alone, never unaided and never forgotten. He will come to us. All it takes is for us to be still.

It is "God's past" that provides calm for "our future." Know that he is God! Know it, not merely intellectually, but practically, spiritually, and emotionally. He is our God. He is the ruler of kingdoms of this earth and the all-powerful Creator of the Universe. "Be still, and know that I am God."

Notes: _____

_____

_____

_____

_____

_____

_____

_____

_____

_____

_____

_____

_____

_____

_____

_____

_____

_____

Be Thankful

1 Thessalonians 5:18 (NLT)

Be thankful in all circumstances, for this is God's will for you who belong to Christ Jesus.

1 Thessalonians 5:18 (KJV)

In everything give thanks: for this is the will of God in Christ Jesus concerning you.

I'm sure most, if not all of us, have heard the song "Every Day Is a Day of Thanksgiving." The chorus goes:

Every day is a day of thanksgiving.

God's been so good to me, everyday He's blessing me.

Every day is a day of thanksgiving;

Take the time to glorify the Lord today.

If you were asked what you are most thankful for, what would you say? Many people start with being thankful for life, relationships, children, and/or jobs. But what can believers be thankful for when persecution threatens life, marriages break up, children become prodigals, unemployment looms, or food becomes rationed?

The Apostle Paul learned the meaning of true thanksgiving, even in the midst of great adversity. He was separated from friends, unjustly accused, and brutally treated.

If ever a person had a right to complain, it was this man, languishing – almost forgotten – in a harsh Roman prison. But instead of complaints, his mouth was filled with words of praise and thanksgiving!

Earlier, when he had been imprisoned in Rome, Paul wrote, "Sing and make music in your heart to the Lord, always giving thanks to God the Father for everything, in the name of our Lord Jesus Christ" (Ephesians 5:19-20, NIV).

Paul was always giving thanks for everything no matter the circumstances. Thanksgiving for the Apostle Paul was not a once-a-year celebration, but a daily reality that changed his life and made him a joyful person in every situation.

Thanksgiving, the giving of thanks to God for all His blessings, should be one of the most distinctive marks of the believer in Jesus Christ. We must not allow a spirit of ingratitude to harden our heart and chill our relationship with God and with others.

Nothing turns us into bitter, selfish, dissatisfied people more quickly than an ungrateful heart. And nothing will do more to restore contentment and the joy of our salvation than a true spirit of thankfulness.

In the Old Testament, leprosy was a terrible disease. It hopelessly disfigured those who had it, and it permanently cut them off from normal society. Without exception, every leper yearned for one thing: To be healed.

One day, ten lepers approached Jesus outside a village, loudly pleading with Him to heal them. Instantly, Jesus restored them all to perfect health, but only one returned and thanked Him. The other nine left without a word of thanks, their minds preoccupied only with themselves.

Today, ingratitude and thanklessness are far too common. Children forget to thank their parents for all that they do. Adults forget to thank each other for what they do. Common courtesy is scorned. Some of us take for granted the ways that others help us. Above all, we fail to thank God for His blessings.

Ingratitude is a sin, just as surely as is lying or stealing or immorality or any other sin condemned by the Bible. (Romans 1:21, NIV) "Although they knew God, they neither glorified him as God nor gave thanks to him."

An ungracious heart is a heart that is cold toward God and indifferent to His mercy and love. It is a heart that has forgotten how dependent we are on God for everything.

From one end of the Bible to the other, we are commanded to be thankful. In fact, thankfulness is the natural outflowing of a heart that is attuned to God. The psalmist declared, "Sing to the Lord with thanksgiving" (Psalm 147:7, NIV). Paul wrote, "Be thankful" (Colossians 3:15, NIV).

Why should we be thankful? Because God has blessed us, and we should be thankful for each blessing. A spirit of thanksgiving is always the mark of a joyous Christian.

As Christians, we should be thankful for being chosen.

Have you ever been the first person chosen to be on a team? When you're picked first, there's a sense of achievement and respect that you bring along. God chose us out of our sinful lifestyle and gave purpose for our life. Thank God today that you were chosen to receive the forgiveness of sins and a place among those called by Him.

"In him we were also chosen, having been predestined according to the plan of him who works out everything in conformity with the purpose of his will" (Ephesians 1:11).

We should be thankful for peace in the midst of storms.

Storms will come whether in the form of an illness, persecution, financial distress, family problems or in other situations. Sooner or later your faith will be tested and you will need peace that transcends understanding. This peace is available to all believers. Through the Holy Spirit, there's an assurance of the peace of God in any storm. Thank God today that you can have peace in the midst of great stress and trials.

"And the peace of God, which transcends all understanding, will guard your hearts and your minds in Christ Jesus" (Philippians 4:7).

We should be thankful that all things work together for our good.

It's a spiritual puzzle you may never understand in this lifetime. God knows how to put together key moments of time, people, and situations to work out the best interests of those who love Him. God can turn the worst possible situations for His glory and your best outcome. Thank God today that He is working every puzzle piece of your life for your good.

"And we know that in all things God works for the good of those who love him, who have been called according to his purpose" (Romans 8:28).

We should be thankful for the love that God has for us.

It's distressing to know that many people live without really feeling loved when God loves them with an unconditional love. We're so loved by God that He sent His one and only Son, Jesus Christ, to take the penalty for our sins. There is nothing we can do to make Him love us more nor less. Thank God today for the abundant love that He shows every day.

"This is love: not that we loved God, but that he loved us and sent his Son as an atoning sacrifice for our sins" (1 John 4:10).

We should be thankful that God listens to us.

Isn't it amazing that despite all the activity in the world, the Creator listens to us? Have you ever noticed how people act in the presence of politicians and famous individuals? How much greater it is to have entrance into the throne room of God at any time? It's a privilege that's easy to take for granted. Thank God today for the awesome greatness of being heard from the Most High Father in heaven.

"This is the confidence we have in approaching God: that if we ask anything according to his will, he hears us. And if we know that he hears us—whatever we ask—we know that we have what we asked of him" (1 John 5:14-15).

We should be thankful that we are never alone.

We have the presence of God at all times whether we sense it or not. Through the Holy Spirit, every believer can have continual contact with God at all times. There's nothing ever hidden from His eyes. Even in the darkest hours when all seems lost—He's there. Thank God today that you are never alone in Him.

"And surely I am with you always, to the very end of the age" (Matthew 28:20).

We should be thankful that heaven is our true home.

The trials of life often remind us that we have a heavenly dwelling with no sorrow, tears, or hardship. It's a place of eternal joy, peace, and love. Our joyful expectation is to be reunited with loved ones and, most of all, to see Jesus as He is and worship Him in the presence of the angels. Thank God today for your heavenly home after your time on this earth. "But our citizenship is in heaven" (Philippians 3:20). Give thanks today.

When we are in a season of suffering, it may be difficult to be thankful. By the grace of God, your eyes can be opened to always find something to thank Him for. If you are a believer in the Lord Jesus Christ, you can be thankful even in times of distress, no matter who you are, where you live, or what you do in life. Be thankful.

Notes: _____

_____

_____

_____

_____

_____

_____

_____

_____

_____

_____

Become What You Are

Romans 12:1–2 (ESV)

[1]I appeal to you therefore, brothers, by the mercies of God, to present your bodies as a living sacrifice, holy and acceptable to God, which is your spiritual worship. [2]Do not be conformed to this world, but be transformed by the renewal of your mind, that by testing you may discern what is the will of God, what is good and acceptable and perfect.

The aim or purpose of Romans 12:1–2 is that all of life would become "spiritual worship." Verse 1 reads, "Present your bodies as a living sacrifice, holy and acceptable to God, which is your spiritual worship." The aim or purpose of all human life in God's eyes is that Christ would be made to look as valuable as he is. Worship means using our minds and hearts and bodies to express the worth of God and all he is for us in Jesus. There is a way to live, a way to love that does that. There is a way to do your job that expresses the true value of God. If you can't find it, that may mean you should change jobs. Or it might mean that verse 2 is not happening to the degree it should.

Verse 2 is Paul's answer to how we turn all of life into worship. We must be transformed. Not just our external behavior, but the way we feel and think. [2]"Be transformed by the renewal of your mind."

Those who believe in Christ Jesus are already blood-bought new creatures in Christ. "If anyone is in Christ, he is a new creation" (2 Corinthians 5:17). But now we must become what we are. "Cleanse out the old leaven that you may be a new lump, as you really are unleavened" (1 Corinthians 5:7).

"You *have* put on the new self, which is being renewed in knowledge after the image of its creator" (Colossians 3:10). You have been made new in Christ; and now you are being renewed day by day.

Now we focus on the last part of verse 2, namely, the aim of the renewed mind: "Do not be conformed to this world, but be transformed by the renewal of your mind, [now here comes the aim] that by testing you may discern what the will of God is, what is good and acceptable and perfect." So our focus today is on the meaning of the term "will of God" and how we discern it.

The Two Wills of God

There are two clear and very different meanings for the term "will of God" in the Bible. We need to know them and decide which one is being used here in Romans 12:2. In fact, knowing the difference between these two meanings of "the will of God" is crucial to understanding one of the biggest and most perplexing things in all the Bible, namely, that God is sovereign over all things and yet disapproves of many things. This means that God disapproves of some of what he ordains to happen. That is, he forbids some of the things he brings about. And he commands some of the things he hinders. Or to put it most paradoxically: God wills some events in one sense that he does not will in another sense.

1. God's Will of Decree, or Sovereign Will

Let's see the passages of Scripture that make us think this way. First consider passages that describe "the will of God" as his sovereign control of all that comes to pass. One of the clearest is the way Jesus spoke of the will of God in Gethsemane when he was praying. He said, in Matthew 26:39, "My Father, if it be possible, let this cup pass from me; nevertheless, not as I will, but as you will." What does the will of God refer to in this verse? It refers to the sovereign plan of God that will happen in the coming hours. You recall how Acts 4:27–28 says this: "Truly in this city there were gathered together against your holy servant Jesus, whom you anointed, both Herod and Pontius Pilate, along with the Gentiles and the peoples of Israel, to do whatever your hand and your plan had predestined to take place." Therefore the "will of God" was that Jesus die. This was his plan, his decree. There was no changing it, and Jesus bowed and said, "Here's my request, but you do what is best to do." That's the sovereign will of God.

Don't miss the very crucial point here, that it includes the sins of man. Herod, Pilate, the soldiers, the Jewish leaders – they all sinned in fulfilling God's will that his Son be crucified (Isaiah 53:10). So be very clear on this: God wills (allows to come to pass) some things that he hates.

In 1 Peter 3:17, Peter writes, "It is better to suffer for doing good, if that should be God's will, than for doing evil." In other words, it may be God's will that Christians suffer for doing good. He has in mind persecution. But persecution of Christians who do not deserve it is sin. So again, God sometimes wills that events come about that include sin. "It is better to suffer for doing good, if that should be God's will."

Paul gives a sweeping summary statement of this truth in Ephesians 1:11. "In him [Christ] we have obtained an inheritance, having been predestined according to the purpose of him who works all things according to the counsel of his will." The will of God is God's sovereign governance of all that comes to pass. There are many other passages in the Bible that teach that God's providence over the universe extends to the smallest details of nature and human decisions. "Not one sparrow falls to the ground apart from our Father in heaven" (Matthew 10:29). "The lot is cast into the lap, but its every decision is from the Lord" (Proverbs 16:33). "The plans of the heart belong to man, but the answer of the tongue is from the Lord" (Proverbs 16:1). "The king's heart is a stream of water in the hand of the Lord; he turns it wherever he will" (Proverbs 21:1).

That's the first meaning of the will of God: It is God's sovereign control of all things. We will call this his "sovereign will" or his "will of decree." It cannot be broken. It always comes to pass. "He does according to his will among the host of heaven and among the inhabitants of the earth; and none can stay his hand or say to him, 'What have you done?'" (Daniel 4: 35).

2. God's Will of Command

Now the other meaning for "the will of God" in the Bible is what we can call his "will of command." His will is what he commands us to do. This is the will of God we can disobey and fail to do. The will of decree we do whether we believe in it or not. The will of command we can fail to do. For example, Jesus said, "Not everyone who says to

96

me, 'Lord, Lord,' will enter the kingdom of heaven, but the one who does the will of my Father who is in heaven" (Matthew 7:21). Not all do the will of his Father. He says so. "Not everyone will enter the kingdom of heaven." Why? Because not all do the will of God.

Paul says in 1 Thessalonians 4:3, "This is the will of God, your sanctification: that you abstain from sexual immorality." Here we have a very specific instance of what God commands of us: holiness, sanctification, sexual purity. This is his will of command. But, oh, so many do not obey.

Then Paul says in 1 Thessalonians 5:18, "Give thanks in all circumstances; for this is the will of God in Christ Jesus for you." There again is a specific aspect of his will of command: Give thanks in all circumstances. But many do not do this will of God.

One more example: "And the world is passing away along with its desires, but whoever does the will of God abides forever" (1 John 2:17). Not all abide forever. Some do. Some don't. The difference? Some do the will of God. Some don't. The will of God, in this sense, does not always happen.

I conclude from these and many other passages of the Bible that there are two ways of talking about the will of God. Both are true, and both are important to understand and believe in. One we can call God's will of decree (or his sovereign will) and the other we can call God's will of command. His will of decree always comes to pass whether we believe in it or not. His will of command can be broken, and is, every day.

The Preciousness of These Truths

Before I relate this to Romans 12:2, let me comment on how precious these two truths are. Both correspond to a deep need that we all have when we are deeply hurt or experience great loss. On the one hand, we need the assurance that God is in control and, therefore, is able to work all the pain and loss together for the good of all who love him. On the other hand, we need to know that God empathizes with us and does not delight in sin or pain in and of themselves. These two needs correspond to God's will of decree and his will of command.

For example, if you were badly abused as a child, and someone asks if you think that was the will of God, you now have a way to make some biblical sense out of this and give an answer that doesn't contradict the Bible. You may say, "No it was not God's will; because he commands that humans not be abusive, but love each other." The abuse broke his commandment and therefore moved his heart with anger and grief (Mark 3:5). In one sense, it was God's will (his sovereign will) because there are a hundred ways he could have stopped it. For reasons I don't yet fully understand, he didn't.

And corresponding to these two wills are the two things you need in this situation: one is a God who is strong and sovereign enough to turn it for good; and the other is a God who is able to empathize with you. On the one hand, Christ is a sovereign High King, and nothing happens apart from his will (Matthew 28:18). On the other hand, Christ is a merciful High Priest and sympathizes with our weaknesses and pain (Hebrews 4:15). The Holy Spirit conquers us and our sins when he wills (John 1:13; Romans 9:15–16) and allows himself to be quenched and grieved and angered when he wills (Ephesians 4:30; 1 Thessalonians 5:19). His sovereign will is invincible, and his will of command can be grievously broken.

We need both these truths, both these understandings of the will of God, not only to make sense out of the Bible, but to hold fast to God in suffering.

Which Will Is Referred to in Romans 12:2?

Now, which of these is meant in Romans 12:2, which reads, "Do not be conformed to this world, but be transformed by the renewal of your mind, that by testing you may discern what is the will of God, what is good and acceptable and perfect." The answer surely is that Paul is referring to God's will of command. I say this for at least two reasons. One is that God does not intend for us to know most of his sovereign will ahead of time. "The secret things belong to the Lord our God, but the things that are revealed belong to us" (Deuteronomy 29:29). If you want to know the future details of God's will of decree, you don't want a renewed mind, you want a crystal ball. This is not called transformation and obedience; it's called divination, soothsaying.

The other reason I say that the will of God in Romans 12:2 is God's will of command, and not his will of decree, is that the phrase "by testing you may discern," implies that we should approve of the will of God and then obediently do it. But, in fact, we should not approve of sin or do it, even though it is part of God's sovereign will. Paul's meaning in Romans 12:2 is paraphrased almost exactly in Hebrews 5:14, which says, "Solid food is for the mature, for those who have their powers of discernment trained by constant practice to distinguish good from evil." (See another paraphrase in Philippians 1:9–11.) That's the goal of this verse: not ferreting out the *secret* will of God that he *plans* to do, but discerning the *revealed* will of God that we *ought* to do.

Three Stages of Knowing and Doing the Revealed Will of God

There are three stages of knowing and doing the revealed will of God – his will of command. All of them require the renewed mind with its Holy-Spirit-given discernment that was discussed last time.

First, God's will of command is revealed with final, decisive authority only in the Bible. We need the renewed mind to understand and embrace what God commands in the Scripture. Without the renewed mind, we will distort the Scriptures to avoid their radical commands for self-denial, love, and purity, and supreme satisfaction in Christ alone. God's authoritative will of command is found only in the Bible. Paul says that the Scriptures are inspired and make the Christian "competent, equipped for every good work" (2 Timothy 3:16–17). Not just some good works. "Every good work." Oh, what energy and time and devotion Christians should spend meditating on the written Word of God.

The second stage of God's will of command is our application of the biblical truth to new situations, that may or may not be explicitly addressed in the Bible. The Bible does not tell you which person to marry, which car to drive, whether to own a home, where you take your vacation, what cell phone plan to buy, which brand of orange juice to drink, nor a thousand other choices you must make.

What is necessary is that we have a renewed mind, which is shaped and governed by the revealed will of God in the Bible; that we see and assess all relevant factors with the mind of Christ; and that we discern what God is calling us to do. This is very different from constantly trying to hear God's voice saying do this and do that. People who try to lead their lives by hearing voices are not in sync with Romans 12:2.

There is a world of difference between praying and laboring for a renewed mind that discerns how to apply God's Word on the one hand, and the habit of asking God to give you a new revelation of what to do on the other hand. Divination does not require transformation. God's aim is a new mind, a new way of thinking and judging, not just new information. His aim is that we be transformed, sanctified, freed by the truth of his revealed Word (John 8:32; 17:17). Therefore, the second stage of God's will of command is the discerning application of the Scriptures to new situations in life, by means of a renewed mind.

Finally, the third stage of God's will of command is the vast majority of living where there is no conscious reflection before we act. I venture to say that a good 95% of your behavior, you do not premeditate. That is, most of your thoughts, attitudes, and actions are spontaneous. They are just spillovers from what's inside. Jesus said, [34]"...out of the abundance of the heart the mouth speaks. [35]The good person out of his good treasure brings forth good, and the evil person out of his evil treasure brings forth evil. [36]I tell you, on the Day of Judgment, people will give account for every careless word they speak" (Matthew 12:34–36).

Why do I call this part of God's will of command? For one reason. God commands things like: Don't be angry. Don't be prideful. Don't covet. Don't be anxious. Don't be jealous. Don't envy. And none of those actions are premeditated. Anger, pride, covetousness, anxiety, jealousy, envy — they all rise up out of the heart with no conscious reflection or intention. We are guilty because of them. They break the commandment of God.

Is it not plain, therefore, that there is one great task of the Christian life: Be transformed by the renewing of your mind. We need new hearts and new minds. "Make the tree good and the fruit will be good..." (Matthew 12:33). That's the great challenge. That is what God calls you to. You can't do it on your own. You need Christ, who died for your sins. And you need the Holy Spirit to lead you into Christ-exalting truth and to work in you, truth-embracing humility.

Give yourself to this: immerse yourself in the written Word of God and saturate your mind with it. Pray that the Spirit of Christ will make you so new that the spillover would be good, acceptable, perfect, and the will of God.

Notes: _____

_____

_____

_____

_____

_____

_____

_____

_____

_____

_____

_____

_____

_____

_____

A Sacrifice for Sin

2 Corinthians 5:21 (NIV)

For He made Him who knew no sin to be sin for us, that we might become the righteousness of God in Him.

2 Corinthians 6:2 (NIV)

In the time of my favor I heard you, and in the day of salvation I helped you." I tell you, now is the time of God's favor, now is the day of salvation.

Christ was made of a woman, took flesh of a sinful woman; though the flesh he took of her was not sinful, being sanctified by the Spirit of God, the former of Christ's human nature: however, he appeared "in the likeness of sinful flesh;" being attended with infirmities, the effects of sin, though sinless; and he was traduced by men as a sinner, and treated as such. He was made a sacrifice for sin, in order to make expiation and atonement for sin.

To be made the righteousness of God is to be made righteous in the sight of God, by the imputation of the righteousness of Christ. Just as Christ is made sin, or a sinner, by the imputation of the sins of others to him; so they are made righteousness, or righteous persons, through the imputation of his righteousness to them; and in no other way can the one be made sin, or the other righteousness.

Christ's righteousness is unto all, and upon all them that believe, it is imputed to them, and put upon them; it is not anything wrought in them; it is not inherent in them. "Surely in the Lord have I righteousness and strength" (Isaiah 45:24).

For us to understand, this mystery needs a revelation, the exchange that took place at Calvary.

In our Christian walk, the moment we realize that we are the righteousness of God, it puts you above situations in life and you begin to walk in this newness of life. You wouldn't want to go back and pick up your sins and live in sin again.

One of the great biblical texts on salvation is 2 Corinthians 5:21. There we see the partnership of the Father and Son producing our rescue. (1 Peter 2:24) First, all of our sins were placed on Christ, who bore them on the cross on our behalf. (John1:12). Then, Christ's right standing with the Father is given to those who trust Him by faith. Now we are no longer enemies of God, for we have been brought to the Father by the Son's work for us. God demonstrated His love for us when He gave up His one and only Son.

Our righteousness was like filthy rags. There was nothing we could do to make ourselves holy. Thank God, Jesus took our place and did the work for us. It is through his substitutionary work that we have become the righteousness of God through him.

2 Corinthians 6:2 (NIV) "In the time of my favor I heard you, and in the day of salvation I helped you." I tell you, now is the time of God's favor; now is the day of salvation.

Paul now quotes from Isaiah 49:8. If we go back and study that chapter, we find that God is in controversy with His people because of their rejection of the Messiah.

Isaiah 49:8 reads, "Thus says the LORD: 'In an acceptable time I have heard You, And in the day of salvation I have helped You; I will preserve You and give You As a covenant to the people, To restore the earth, To cause them to inherit the desolate heritages.'"

In your time of study, go back and read Isaiah Chapter 49. In verse 7 of that chapter, the Lord is rejected by the nation, and we know that his rejection led to His death. Then in verse 8 we have the words of Jehovah, assuring the Lord Jesus that His prayer has been heard and that God would help and preserve Him.

In the day of salvation, "I helped you" refers to the resurrection of the Lord Jesus Christ. The acceptable time and the day of salvation would be ushered in by Christ's resurrection from among the dead.

In his preaching of the gospel, Paul seized upon his marvelous truth and announces to his unsaved listeners, "Behold, now is the accepted time; behold, now is the day of salvation." In other words, the era of which Isaiah had prophesied as the day of salvation has already come, so Paul urges men to trust the Savior while it is still the day of salvation.

Have you ever wondered why people take risks in trying to catch an elevator when the door is closing, or to get on a train, or at an airport to get to the terminal while the door is closing? You are willing to risk getting hurt when you know another elevator or train will come within a few minutes!

There is a far more important door that we must enter before it closes. It is the door of God's mercy. The apostle Paul tells us, "Behold, now is the accepted time; behold, now is the day of salvation" (2 Cor. 6:2). Christ has come, died for our sins, and has risen from the grave. He has opened the way for us to be reconciled to God and has proclaimed for us the day of salvation.

Today is that day. But one day the door of mercy will close. To those who received and served Christ, He will say, "Come, you blessed of My Father, inherit the kingdom prepared for you" (Matt. 25:34). But those who don't know Him will be turned away (v. 46).

Within this heavenly cluster of fruits, just ripe for you to enjoy from the vineyard of God, you will find that the word *favor* is mentioned twice. Favor is a very strong word.

Now let us go back to our verse for today and see something develop. To begin with, God says, "In the time of my favor I heard you." God hears your prayers and His favor is smiling towards you to answer them. Then, "In the day of salvation I helped you." God gives you His Divine intervention on your behalf to help you. Wow! How amazing is that?

"Now is the time of God's favor, now is the day of salvation." All you will ever need in life is to be found in Jesus Christ, and salvation through Him. Salvation is an all-inclusive meaning to save, rescue, deliver, heal, prosper, protect, and set free.

To experience God's favor through salvation is to know more of His grace, His love and mercy. Grace is God's unmerited favor; it is something that cannot be earned because His grace is a gift. The Bible says in Proverbs 8:35 (NIV), "For whoever finds me finds life and

receives the favor of the LORD." The Hebrew word for favor is *rason* meaning acceptance, goodwill, desires to bless. God's desire is to bless you with His favor, His goodwill over your life, His generosity, and His approval for you to benefit from His blessing over your life through Jesus Christ, the Author of your salvation.

The more you explore our text for today in 2 Corinthians 6:2, the more you see God's desire to bless you in every area of your life. In the Old Testament, people sought the favor of God, but now His favor is willingly being poured over your life as you walk in a covenant relationship with God. The Bible says in the book of Leviticus 26:9 (NIV), "I will look on you with favor and make you fruitful." May you live this day in His favor of salvation and enjoy the benefits that come by living in a covenant relationship with Jesus Christ.

Our response to Jesus Christ determines our destiny. In John 10:9, Jesus invites, "I am the door. If anyone enters by Me, he will be saved." God wants us to be very attentive to him and he wants us to call on Him and find Him at any acceptable time. The fact is that all times are acceptable in the sight of the Lord, but we must make ourselves available. We must spend quality time with God so we can become what God wants and not become what we want.

The Bible tells us that we can experience God's favor in very practical ways. Psalm 5:12 says, "For you, O Lord, will bless the righteous; with favor you will surround him as with a shield." The word "favor" means: (1) to approve or support, (2) to facilitate or help, (3) advantage, benefit, preference. What an awesome thought that the God of Creation wants to "favor you" and shield you with His blessings and guidance! He wants to open doors, connect you with key people, and help you fulfill your destiny. As we examine the subject of God's favor, it's important to grasp two main concepts. The first is what we might call the "positional side" of things. The Bible teaches that in Christ you are already blessed. Ephesians 1:3: That in Christ *"you have been blessed with all spiritual blessings in heavenly places.*" It's important for you to realize that from God's point of view, you already have His favor and blessing. What a wonderful starting point! You can count on this fact, not because of your goodness, but because of what Jesus did for you. His sacrifice paid the price. God's favor is not something you can earn – it's a free benefit that comes with salvation. However, that's not the end of the story. There's also an **"experiential side"** of things to consider as well. Just because something is promised or declared in the Bible doesn't mean that you will automatically experience it. I've seen some Christians try to claim God's favor while they are lazy, showing up late to work, bitter over some past event, and in general not walking In God's favor, but walking in the flesh. The Bible teaches that walking in the flesh will short-circuit God's blessings (Galatians 6:8). This study is dedicated to helping you walk in the "experiential" dimension of God's favor.

Joseph's Life – Keys to Favor

The life of Joseph is a great study on God's favor and success. His story is a classic example of how someone can face unbelievable rejection and setbacks and still come out on top with God's favor. I'm sure you remember the story. As a young boy, Joseph was sold by his own brothers into slavery (Gen 37). Can you imagine the horrible rejection and hurt that an event like that could produce? I'm sure that Joseph was tempted to be bitter just like anyone would. Yet, when you read the whole story, there's no mention of bitterness or a desire for revenge. In fact, it's quite the opposite. Joseph seems to have risen above the hurt through His faith in God's destiny for his life. The Bible says that when his brothers sold him, the slave traders put him in chains and took him down to Egypt (Gen 39; Ps 105:17-22). There, he was sold again and ended up in Potiphar's house. At that horrible time in his life, look at what Genesis 39:2-4 says about Joseph: "And the Lord was with Joseph, and he was a prosperous man; and he was in the house of his master the Egyptian. And his master saw that the Lord was with him and that the Lord made all that he did to prosper in his hand. And Joseph found FAVOR in his sight, and he served him; and he made him overseer over his house and all that he had put into his hand."

Keep in mind that this was said of Joseph when he was a slave and owned absolutely nothing. Prosperous? Favor? This one passage alone confirms that God's view of prosperity and success is far different than the world's view. **In God's mind, "prosperity" is all about who you are on the inside, not what you have on the outside.** God looked upon Joseph's faith and attitude and called him "prosperous." And because he was prosperous on the inside, it was just a matter of time until he experienced God's favor and blessing on the outside. Never forget that prosperity is first and foremost who you are on the inside. Building on Joseph's example, let's look at a powerful key that is generally overlooked regarding God's favor. I have come to believe that this is the MAIN KEY to the "experiential" side of God's favor. In Joseph's story, we see him time and again **"working as to the lord and not unto man."**

No matter what Joseph was asked to do, in his heart he worked as though he was working for the Lord. In Joseph's mind, his boss was the Lord – not Potiphar, Pharaoh, or the jailer. Christians need to grasp this powerful principle and never forget it. It will cure laziness and slackness. God is your "boss" – not an individual, a company, or a government. Thus, whether your current job is washing dishes, working in a factory, cleaning bathrooms, or conducting business in a private jet – **your attitude should be that you are working "unto the Lord" and not for man.** This one simple key will revolutionize the most mundane tasks. It will turn everything you do into "faith-seeds." It's really the law of sowing and reaping on steroids! **You should work as unto the Lord and expect your promotion to come from Him (Col. 3:23-25).** Keep in mind that when you do this, you are not "earning" God's blessing. Instead, it is simply a powerful way to release your faith and put your expectation in what God alone can do. Joseph did not just sit around bemoaning his plight like most of us would have done. We would have blamed our evil brothers for the rest of our lives! Yet we are told that Joseph quickly got to work wherever he found himself. **He had a deep confidence in the dreams that God**

had given him as a young boy (Gen. 37:5). Joseph refused to let circumstances rob him of his faith and destiny.

Jesus was the sacrifice for our sins. We must continue the Work God has called us to do. Don't let circumstances rob you of your faith and destiny.

Notes_____

_____

_____

_____

_____

_____

_____

_____

_____

_____

_____

_____

_____

_____

Experiencing an Unchanging God in a Changing World

Hebrews 13:8 (NKJV)

[8]Jesus Christ *is* the same yesterday, today, and forever.

In verse 8, the Scripture says that Christ is the same yesterday, today, and forever. Yesterday, meaning all time past. Today, meaning the time present, and forever, meaning all that is future, from the present time to eternity.

The Lord is our unchanging refuge and strength in this rapidly changing world. He is our anchor when we face many changes which can affect us deeply. We can experience such changes in our home, workplace, relationships, nature, finances, health, culture, fashion, laws, government, status, and yes, even people. Sometimes changes can be sudden and traumatic. In these times of changes and disturbances, we must rely on the unchanging God who is our sure foundation. The Lord will be our faithful friend and guide us through these periods of change and uncertainty. The Lord is our unchanging refuge and strength in all the situations that we may face in our life. He is our sure and steadfast companion. He has promised never to leave us nor forsake us.

The Lord Jesus knew that during His experience on the cross, everyone including all His disciples would forsake Him, but He had the assurance that His heavenly Father would be with Him even in that time of loneliness. We can trust the Lord to be with us, even when everyone else has abandoned us.

The Lord is our unchanging refuge and strength even when the hearts of people change, and their love turns to hate. The love of God never changes. The hearts and the faces of people can change, and they may turn against us. People who used to love us and favor us may change their attitudes suddenly. But the Lord will always be gracious to us and look on us with favor. His love is unchanging towards us.

The most powerful weapon against fear and worry is Scripture. You can find a Scripture that pertains to your many circumstances no matter what they are and lean on their power to reassure you. But why are the words of the Bible so much more powerful than others? It's because the Word of God has been unchangeable down through the centuries, unchangeable and reliable at all times.

The God who delivered the Israelites yesterday will deliver you today and your children tomorrow. God's love, power and almighty presence is unceasing. What a wonderful and reassuring feeling! Malachi 3:6 says: "For I am the Lord, I do not change."

Change happens all around us; day changes to night, the seasons change, and the circumstances of our lives change. One day we may be up and the next day, down. Even those who love us most may change as the days, weeks, and years pass. God was wise enough to understand that we are human and that change in our lives should be part of the human condition, yet he also gave us certain constants in our lives. Yes, there are seasons, but they follow a predictable pattern so that crops can grow and we can appreciate the beauty of nature. Day always follows night so that we can rest when we need to and wake up each day feeling refreshed. There is a *constancy* to even the changes in our lives that tell us that God's love is always present.

Knowing that our universe is put together so that we can rely on it to follow a reliable pattern is reassuring. It tells us that God himself is constant in His love for us, so we need not fear. His loving kindness is eternal and never changing. Even as our lives change, jobs come and go, and relationships grow and fade, God is steadfastly loving us and watching over us. 1 Peter 5:7: "Give all your worries to God, for he cares what happens to you."

When something in our lives goes wrong or brings us sorrow, we sometimes tell ourselves, "Don't worry, this too shall pass." It is a thought that helps us to feel just a little bit better about the lows in our lives, but when the highs come along, we don't want to think that they are only temporary. It is reassuring to remember that God has promised to always be there. He is not temporary, and His love will never pass away from our lives.

God's love, power and protection are never changing and never-ending, no matter what we do or what happens in the universe. We don't have to tell ourselves that things will change when we think about God. He's always been there and always will be. God's mighty presence is with us in all circumstances and conditions, in all places at all times. Any adversity that we face gives God another opportunity for us to experience His great peace, love and understanding. How wonderful that the Lord is so constant – you never have to worry about whether He is there for you or not! He is eternal, just as He has always said.

Deuteronomy 31:8 says, "Do not be afraid or discouraged, for the Lord is the one who goes before you. He will be with you; he will neither fail you nor forsake you."

Jesus Christ is our Eternal Lord and God and Savior. His essence, Power and Authority remain the same even before the beginning of all things, both those in Heaven and on earth and beneath the earth or the sea. Though all things shall pass, He is an Everlasting God. He is known as the Mighty God and Everlasting Father (Isaiah 9:6), meaning He ever existed and created all things in His power (John 1:1-3, Colossians 1:16). He is the Sustainer of all things (Colossians 1:17), without Him nothing will exist, including dark spirits. He is the Savior of the world (Redeemer). He is the only Loving God who laid His life down to save all men from the death penalty of their sins when everybody had gone astray (Isaiah 53:4-6). Behold, the Lamb of God, who takes away the sin of the world! (John 1:29). He is the Supreme Judge for all humans (Matthew 25:31-46), and the Sovereign Lord Who is to come and reward the good deeds of men, and punish men for their wickedness (Revelation 22:12-13).

What distinguishes God from man is that man often changes his mind because he cannot foresee all that is coming. God, on the other hand, always foresees what is coming and changes his mind only in response to that foreseen situation. There is a kind of permanence in God that is not in man.

It's not just that God is constantly loving, righteous, wise, and powerful in all circumstances, but also that he knows perfectly how that love, righteousness, wisdom, and power will respond in every circumstance. What makes God different from man is that he does not change his mind because of unforeseen circumstances.

I stress this because when Hebrews 13:8 says, "Jesus Christ is the same yesterday, today and forever," and says it in view of calling Christ "God" in Hebrews 1:8, I want everyone to feel the full weight of this blessing in our lives. The verse is meant to be a powerful incentive to live a certain way at the end of the twentieth century (and every other time). I want it to have all the power it should have.

"Jesus Christ is the same yesterday, today and forever" does not mean that Christ can't respond differently from day to day, rejoicing with you or over you one day and grieving with you or over you another day. Hebrews 4:15 calls him a "sympathizing High Priest." He can and does respond differently to our different circumstances. But now we see that not only are those responses rooted in a consistent character of love, wisdom, righteousness, and power, but also in a perfect knowledge and plan so that he never changes his mind because of unforeseen circumstances. He is the same in his perfect knowledge and his perfect plan and his perfect execution of that plan in all the details of your life to bring about his glorious goal for all his children.

It's almost a shame to say that what God was saying through that preacher was this is not your first time losing someone close to you. You have lost your mother, father, sister, brother, a son, and a host of other relatives.

The same God that brought you through those deaths is the same God who will get you through this death. He is the same God. The same God that was there yesterday is the same God here today.

Jesus Christ is the same yesterday, today and forever - the same truth and the same treasure. Receive him and be free.

Notes: _____

_____

_____

_____

_____

_____

_____

_____

_____

_____

_____

_____

_____

_____

_____

_____

_____

_____

_____

_____

_____

_____

Follow Jesus

Matthew 16:24-26 (NKJV)

[24]"Then Jesus said to His disciples, 'If anyone desires to come after Me, let him deny himself, and take up his cross, and follow Me. [25] For whoever desires to save his life will lose it, but whoever loses his life for My sake will find it. [26] For what profit is it to a man if he gains the whole world, and loses his own soul? Or what will a man give in exchange for his soul?'"

Hebrew's 13:7: Remember those who rule over you, who have spoken the word of God to you, whose faith follow, considering the outcome of their conduct.

The Holy Spirit calls us to remember our leaders, but not just any leaders. He asks us to remember those leaders who taught us the Word of Truth and who were exceptional Christians. God is calling us to follow someone who has a proven Christian life.

This is not just any leader. It's a leader who has taught you the Word. It's a leader whose life has been carefully evaluated over time. When you become saved, there are some friends and some family you have to let go of because they are not following Jesus. They are going in a different direction.

Babies learn to walk by mimicking their mom and dad. A baby Christian learns to live a life of faith by following another Christian. The only question is how good is the model? If someone mimics you or if you mimic someone else, how good is the copy going to be?

The person must be someone whom you have carefully evaluated. Does he or she model love for strangers, prisoners, and the brethren? Has he or she been a faithful spouse and depends on God to meet their needs? Does he or she have great faith? Great faith is obedient and willing to suffer for Jesus.

Jesus frequently encountered people with spiritual questions. They wanted to know how to live life more fully. They wanted to connect with God. They wanted to love others more deeply and authentically. They wanted to know about death and eternal life. They wanted to experience God's forgiveness for their failures and sins. They wanted to understand how to pray, how to worship, how to understand the words of Scripture.

To such people Jesus frequently offered a simple invitation: "Follow me."

What did he mean by that? **"Take up your cross and follow Me"** means being willing to die in order to follow Jesus. This is called "dying to self." It's a call to absolute surrender.

The invitation is offered as an opportunity to learn from Jesus how to live authentically. The beautiful life Jesus lived, marked by a passionate love for God and a compassion for people, is something we can learn. Humility and forgiveness are traits we can develop. The practices of prayer and worship can be cultivated.

But we need a teacher and an example. Jesus offers to take on that role in our lives.

A Master

If we want to learn how to do something well, whether a craft, or skill, we might apprentice ourselves to a master. We spend time with them. We observe them. We let them instruct and correct us. We seek to model ourselves after them. Craftsmen, artists, and athletes alike hone and perfect their abilities in this way.

The late Dallas Willard, a professor of Philosophy at the University of Southern California, compared following Jesus to becoming the apprentice of a master: "A disciple, or apprentice, is simply someone who has decided to be with another, under appropriate conditions, in order to become capable of doing what that person does or to become what that person is."

What do you do if you want to learn to live life well? Where do you go, if you want to live in a way that corresponds to the way God created human beings to live? You seek out an example of a life that has been lived in that way. This is what Jesus offers when he says, "Follow me."

A Disciple

What it means to follow Jesus—to be his apprentice in learning to live life—is then relatively straightforward. It means that we have come to desire the life he offers. We have determined that Jesus is who he claims to be, and that he is the source of the wisdom and knowledge that we are seeking.

In biblical accounts, Jesus uses hunger and thirst to describe our spiritual longings and portrays himself as the bread of life and the living water. Following Jesus begins with faith and trust in him and his promises, as it would with any teacher.

Following Jesus means being with him. This is not an online course. Christians believe that Jesus Christ died for the sins of humankind but was also resurrected from the dead and thus remains personally available to his followers—available to be known and experienced.

We experience his presence and hear his voice through practices like prayer, worship, and reading the Bible. These practices allow us to intentionally be with our teacher so that we may learn to follow him.

Following Jesus means learning to obey him. Ultimately, what is the point of having an expert teacher if one does not do what the teacher says? We do not follow Jesus by occasionally going to him for advice when we're in pain, but by trusting him as the source of wisdom from which we wish to learn. Take a look at some of Jesus' own words:

[24]"Therefore everyone who hears these words of mine and puts them into practice is like a wise man who built his house on the rock. [25]The rain came down, the streams rose, and the winds blew and beat against that house; yet it did not fall, because it had its foundation on the rock. [26]But everyone who hears these words of mine and does not put them into practice is like a foolish man who built his house on sand. [27]The rain came down, the streams rose, and the winds blew and beat against that house, and it fell with a great crash" (Matthew 7:24-27).

A Directive

The purpose of this apprenticeship, as Dallas Willard often notes, is not to live the life Jesus lived. That has already been done—and we could never be perfect as Jesus was. The purpose is to learn to live your real, present life with all its responsibilities, relationships, and roles as Jesus would live it if it were His.

Then ask yourself am I truly following Jesus? If you think so, then listen to what Jesus said in His Word. But if you are not sure…then hear what Jesus says to you so that you will know for sure.

Next, start to use every means available to learn more about Jesus and to understand his teachings. Reading the four Gospels—Matthew, Mark, Luke, and John—is a good starting point to come to know Jesus and his ways fully.

Finally, understand no one follows Jesus perfectly. But over time, the disciple begins to reflect his master's influence. You have a choice to follow Him or not; and if you choose to follow Jesus, you will have to completely surrender yourself to Him. Following Jesus means there's no chance of getting lost.

Many Christians today who claim to be following Jesus go around talking about Jesus, His love and faith, but they don't want to endure any suffering, partake of His suffering, or do what He has said in His Word as the cost is too great.

Make a decision to follow Jesus. Commit to listening to him, obeying him, and allowing him to shape your life.

Notes: _____

_____

_____

_____

_____

Forgetting the Past, Pressing Toward the Goal

Philippians 3:12-14 NLT

[12]"I don't mean to say that I have already achieved these things or that I have already reached perfection. But I press on to possess that perfection for which Christ Jesus first possessed me. [13]No, dear brothers and sisters, I have not achieved it, but I focus on this one thing: Forgetting the past and looking forward to what lies ahead, [14]I press on to reach the end of the race and receive the heavenly prize for which God, through Christ Jesus, is calling us."

The Apostle Paul did not consider that he was already perfect. Perfected refers not to the resurrection in verse 11, but the whole subject of conformity to Christ. He had no idea that it was possible to achieve a state of sinlessness, or to arrive at a condition in life where no further progress could be achieved. Paul realized that satisfaction is the greatest of progress.

He pressed so that the purpose for which the Lord Jesus had saved him might be fulfilled in him. The Apostle Paul was apprehended by Christ on the road to Damascus. You might ask what the purpose of this momentous meeting was. It was that Paul might from then on, be a pattern - saint, that God might show through him what Christ can do in human life. He was not yet perfectly conformed to Christ. The process was still going on, and Paul was aware that this work of God's grace might continue and deepen.

Philippians 4:1: Not that I speak in regard to need, for I have learned in whatever state I am, to be content.

This man, who had learned to be content with whatever material things he had, never could be content with his spiritual attainments. He did not count himself to have arrived, as we would say today. So, what did he do? He was a man of single purpose. He had one aim and ambition. In this he resembled David, who said, "One thing have I desired of the Lord."

Forgetting those things which are behind would mean not only his sins and failures, but also his natural privileges, attainments, and successes which he had described in this chapter and even his spiritual triumphs.

And reaching forward to those things which are ahead: namely, the privileges and responsibilities of the Christian life, whether worship, service, or the personal development of Christian character.

Looking at himself as a runner in a race, Paul describes himself as exerting every effort **toward the goal for the prize of the upward call of God in Christ Jesus. The goal** is the finish line at the end of the racetrack. **The prize** is the award presented to the winner. Here, the goal would be the finish of life's race and perhaps, more particularly, the Judgement Seat of Christ. The prize would be the crown of righteousness which Paul describes elsewhere for those who have run well.

The upward Call of God in Christ Jesus includes all the purposes that God had in mind when saving us. It includes salvation, conformity to Christ, joint heirship with Him, a home in heaven, and countless other spiritual blessings.

Forgetting those things which are behind so you can reach forward to those things which are ahead (Philippians 3:13) can bring gut-wrenching pain to your soul. Some of us know that pain all too well, and probably have experienced it many times. To describe the process as difficult would be an understatement.

Sometimes moving on feels like leaving a piece of yourself behind. Other times forgetting those things which are behind seems like an exercise in futility. Still, other times reaching forward to those things which are ahead is, well, let's just say you may feel there is a tug of war in your soul threatening to tear you apart.

Forgetting those things which are behind is perhaps one of the greatest challenges we can face, especially when those "things" were a major part of our daily lives. Have you ever had to "forget" a husband, or a wife, best friend, or a ministry and more—and sometimes in the midst of great persecution?

We can forget those things which are behind, or at least we can remember them without the gut-wrenching pain we felt while we were making the transition. And we can press on toward the goal with joy.

Soulish Realities

It all starts in the mind. What we think about can live on as reality in our souls long after a painful event has passed. Have you ever had to part ways with a friend who was always causing problems in the friendship? Maybe you were growing spiritually and the friend was trying to hold you back from your blessings. There are times that you just have to let go. Listen to the Holy Spirit.

Sometimes you have to resist that temptation with everything in you at first. After all, everyone likes a good friend, and nobody wants to hurt a friend. You have to quickly grab hold of the reigns of your mind, stop replaying the scenes over and over again in your mind, and reach forward to those things which are ahead. The only way out is through, and it starts with a disciplined mind.

Maybe it's not a relationship. Maybe you need to forget past hurts, past failures, or even past successes. The point is this: Dwelling on an unpleasant past, no matter how recent or far away that past is, can't lead to healing. Dwelling on an unpleasant past isn't the path to forgiveness. Dwelling on an unpleasant past can't send you to the next place God wants to take you. It just can't! Dwelling on an unpleasant past can only keep you tied to that past, which hinders you from moving forward in God.

Beloved Brothers and Sisters, if you are led by the Spirit of God to end your relationship with a person or place, or if the enemy caused you to experience great loss in your life through death, divorce or some other tragedy, God has something better for you. And if your past is one of shame, guilt, and condemnation for sins you've committed, God is ready, willing, and able to forgive you and cleanse you from all unrighteousness.

Trust for Restoration

Trust God. He will restore anything the enemy stole from your life, and He may even restore relationships with people who walked away from you (or people He told you to walk away from). Our job is not to wonder what could have been or what will be. Our job is to obey God. Be assured, when we don't walk in obedience to the Word, the challenge to forget those things which are behind becomes even greater. He gives grace to those who seek to obey.

God is a progressive God – he's always moving forward. By His grace, and with a will determined not to dwell on an unpleasant past, we can overcome the challenge of forgetting those things that are behind. I won't lie to you; it won't be easy. The past may even come back to "haunt" you sometimes. But the battle really is in the mind. The good news is, you have the mind of Christ (1 Corinthians. 2:16) and God has a good plan for you. Press forward to that goal. Leave the past behind.

One thing is obvious to me. We are closer to eternity. Like the apostle, I haven't "apprehended," i.e., I haven't gotten hold of that which has gotten hold of me. I am still here in this body of carnality; I'm still in the race. I have someone who has run the race before and plotted out the way. If I look to Him, I cannot fail.

Now is the time for resolutions. We must examine ourselves (I Cor. 11:28; II Cor. 13:5; Gal. 6:4) on a daily basis rather than that empty annual ritual. Paul said that he would forget those things which had passed and look to the future.

We must forget past failures as we lay aside the weights and sins that beset us: "The blood of Jesus still avails to cover our sins" (I John 1:7). God looks at us through the blood of Jesus and finds us perfect and complete (Col. 2:10). We are seated in heavenly places with Him (Eph. 2:6). Knowing myself, that's hard to comprehend, but that is a fact.

We must forget past blessings and achievements. While very appreciative, we can't live on yesterday's manna (Exodus 16:20). We need fresh oil from the throne of God today (Psalm 92:10).

We must forget past hurts and snubs from friends. Dwelling on perceived or real hurts and slights does nothing but sap our strength and our joy. We must do our best to amend any bad situation, but having failed that, we still have a race to run. We must quit wasting energy on things that we can't do anything about. Instead, concentrate on the One who holds all power of heaven and earth, upholds all things by the word of His power (Matt. 28:18; Heb. 1:3). We must press towards the mark of the high calling of God in Christ Jesus.

We must continue to look for the coming of Jesus. This is our "blessed hope" (Titus 2:13). We have treasures laid up in heaven (Matt. 6:19), that we can't begin to comprehend (Isa. 64:4; Col. 1:5; 1Co 2; Heb. 11:16). We desire to be found blameless in Him when that day occurs (II Peter 3:14), knowing that we will be rewarded according to our works (Matt. 16:27).

While we're waiting for eternity, we have a job to do in the here and now. We must walk in a godly manner before the people of the world (Col. 4,5; I Thess. 4:12; James 3:13).

God has given us a few short days to walk on this earth, and we must not waste them. We must redeem the time as we labor for His kingdom (Col. 4:5).

Heb. 12:2: Looking unto Jesus the author and finisher of our faith; who for the joy that was set before him endured the cross, despising the shame, and is set down at the right hand of the throne of God.

Let's forget those things in the past that are holding us back from moving forward. May we press forward together towards that high calling of God in Christ Jesus. God bless each and every one of you.

Notes: _____

_____

_____

_____

_____

_____

_____

_____

_____

_____

_____

_____

_____

_____

_____

_____

_____

_____

_____

_____

_____

_____

_____

Forgiveness

Mark 11:25 (NKJV)

[25]And whenever you stand praying, if you have anything against anyone, forgive him, that your Father in heaven may also forgive you your trespasses.

The story of the Prodigal Son, also known as the Parable of the Lost Son, follows the parables of the Lost Sheep and the Lost Coin. Jesus is responding to the Pharisees' complaint: "This man welcomes sinners and eats with them."

Jesus tells the story of a man who has two sons. The younger son asks his father to give him his portion of the family estate as an early inheritance. Once received, the son promptly sets off on a long journey to a distant land and begins to waste his fortune on wild living. When the money runs out, a severe famine hits the country and the son finds himself in dire circumstances. He takes a job feeding pigs. Eventually, he grows so destitute that he even longs to eat the food assigned to the pigs.

The young man finally comes to his senses, remembering his father. In humility, he recognizes his foolishness, decides to return to his father and ask for forgiveness and mercy. As the son made his confession, total forgiveness and restoration of the father/son relationship is indicated in the father's response.

Forgiveness is a huge subject and certainly one in which the Bible is not silent about. In the Bible we can read about our amazing and loving Heavenly Father who forgives us of all trespasses. God calls sinners to seek Him and promises them forgiveness. It is because of His great mercy and grace that God rescues the believer from the dominion of darkness that began way back in the Garden. Jesus extends a loving invitation for forgiveness of sins, which is only possible through His shed blood. He gave His life so that we may live. We are forgiven because He was forsaken. That is amazing love!

Forgiveness is the attitude of forgiving someone who is willing to forgive other people. It could also mean giving up my right to hurt you, for hurting me. It is impossible to live on this fallen planet without getting hurt, offended, misunderstood, lied to, and rejected. Learning how to respond properly is one of the basics of the Christian life.

The word "forgive" means to wipe the slate clean, to pardon, to cancel a debt. When we wrong someone, we should seek his or her forgiveness in order for the relationship to be restored. It is important to remember that forgiveness is not granted because a person deserves to be forgiven. Instead, it is an act of love, mercy, and grace.

How we act toward that person may change. It doesn't mean we will put ourselves back into a harmful situation or that we suddenly accept or approve of the person's continued wrong behavior. It simply means we release them from the wrong they committed against us. We forgive them because God forgave us. Ephesians 4:31 says, "Let all bitterness, wrath, anger, clamor, and evil speaking be put away from you, with all malice." Romans 5:8 says, "God demonstrates His own love towards us, in that while we were still sinners, Christ died for us."

What does God say about forgiveness?

- The Bible gives us a lot of instruction when it comes to forgiveness.

- We forgive because we have been forgiven by God. (Ephesians 4:32): "And be kind to one another, tenderhearted, forgiving one another, even as God in Christ forgave you."

- We forgive in obedience to God (Matthew 6:14-15): [14] "For if you forgive men their trespasses, your heavenly Father will also forgive you. [15] But if you do not forgive men their trespasses, neither will your Father forgive your trespasses."

- We forgive others to gain control of our lives from hurt emotions (Genesis 4:1-8).

- We forgive so we won't become bitter and defile those around us. [14]"Pursue peace with all people, and holiness, without which no one will see the Lord: [15]looking carefully lest anyone fall short of the grace of God; lest any root of bitterness springing up cause trouble, and by this many become defiled" (Hebrews 12:14-15).

What if I don't feel like forgiving others? There are times when we don't feel like forgiving those who have wronged us. It is easier to act our way into feeling than to feel our way into acting. Having a nature of not forgiving others brings about bitterness, and bitterness has been linked to stress-related illnesses by some medical researchers. By forgiving others, we free ourselves spiritually and emotionally. Forgiveness is an act of our own personal will in obedience and submission to God's will, trusting God to bring emotional healing.

Forgiving Others - Direction from God

Romans 3:23: "We have all sinned and deserve God's judgment." God, the Father, sent His only Son to satisfy that judgment for those who believe in Him. Jesus, the creator and eternal Son of God, who lived a sinless life, loves us so much that He died for our sins, taking the punishment that we deserve, was buried, and rose from the dead according to the Bible. If you truly believe and trust this in your heart, receiving Jesus alone as your Savior, declaring, "Jesus is Lord," you will be saved from judgment and spend eternity with God in heaven.

Forgiving others may seem to be a choice, and in one sense it is a choice, but God has been very clear about forgiveness. He has given us specific direction in numerous Scriptures, all of which can be summed up in just one word -- forgive! God's Word in Mark 11:25 says, "And when you stand praying, if you hold anything against anyone, forgive him, so that your Father in heaven may forgive you your sins." Luke 6:37 says, "Do not judge, and you will not be judged. Do not condemn, and you will not be condemned. Forgive, and you will be forgiven"

God is saying that it is in our own best interest to forgive! He is not talking about what is in the best interest of the person who needs to be forgiven. We are the ones who God is trying to protect. We are the ones who receive the most benefit from forgiveness, not the other person. A spirit of unforgiveness complicates and compromises our daily walk with God. Forgiving others release us from anger and allows us to receive the healing we need. The whole reason God has given us specific direction is because He does not want anything to stand between us. God's love for us is beyond our comprehension. Forgiving others spares us from the consequences of living out of an unforgiving heart.

Forgiving others does not carry with it a single decision that we need to ponder. God has not qualified one sin as being more grievous to Him than another, and He has not qualified one sin committed against us as warranting forgiveness and not another. For example, God is not saying, "If a person lies to you or steals from you, you should forgive him, but if they abuse you or harm your child, you can hold them in unforgiveness." He is saying to forgive everyone, always, and do it immediately.

Is Forgive and Forget in The Bible?

The phrase "forgive and forget" is not found in the Bible. However, there are numerous verses commanding us to "forgive one another" (Matthew 6:14).

"For if you forgive men their trespasses, your heavenly Father will also forgive you" (Ephesians 4:32). A Christian who is not willing to forgive others will find his fellowship with God hindered (Matthew 6:15) and can reap bitterness and the loss of reward (Hebrews 12:14–15; 2 John 1:8).

Forgiveness is a decision of the will. Since God commands us to forgive, we must make a conscious choice to obey God and forgive. The offender may not desire forgiveness and may not ever change, but that doesn't negate God's desire that we possess a forgiving spirit (Matthew 5:44). Ideally, the offender will seek reconciliation, but, if not, the one wronged can still decide to forgive.

Of course, it is impossible to truly forget sins that have been committed against us. We cannot selectively "delete" events from our memory. The Bible states that God does not "remember" our wickedness (Hebrews 8:12). But God is still all-knowing. God remembers that we have "sinned and fall short of the glory of God" (Romans 3:23). But, having been forgiven, we are positionally (or judicially) justified. Heaven is ours, as if our sin had never occurred. If we belong to Him through faith in Christ, God does not condemn us for our sins (Romans 8:1). In that sense God "forgives and forgets."

If by "forgive and forget" one means, "I choose to forgive the offender for the sake of Christ and move on with my life," then this is a wise and godly course of action. As much as possible, we should forget what is behind and strive toward what is ahead (Philippians 3:13). We should forgive each other "just as in Christ God forgave" (Ephesians 4:32). We must not allow a root of bitterness to spring up in our hearts (Hebrews 12:15).

Why Should We Forgive?

There is something exquisitely sweet about holding a grudge. The ability to withhold forgiveness and indulge in self-righteous feelings is a heady power. God is the God of justice. Wrongs should be righted. We deserve to feel contempt for those who hurt us, except that it's all a lie. Refusing to forgive doesn't grant us power, it enslaves us to sin. Feeling contempt for others very rarely makes a significant difference in their lives. Absolutely no good whatsoever comes from refusing to forgive. This is why Jesus said we are to forgive one another seventy times seven (Matthew 18:22). We should forgive so much that it becomes second nature—our automatic response to offenses.

God gives us two very good reasons in Scripture for why we should forgive. First, God commands us to forgive others. God forgave us while we were His enemies (Romans 5:10), and we should do likewise with one another. Second, those who do not forgive others indicate that they themselves have not been forgiven because a truly regenerated heart is a forgiving heart (Matthew 6:14-15). If we are filled with resentment and bitterness, we are exhibiting the "works of the flesh," not the fruit of the Spirit, which is evidence of true salvation (Galatians 5:19-23).

Most importantly, when we disobey one of God's commands, such as the command to forgive, we sin against Him. In refusing to forgive another person, we sin against that person, but also against God. Considering that God puts our transgressions as far from Him as the east is from the west (Psalm 103:12), He expects us to extend this same grace to others. Our sin against God is infinitely more vague and easily noticed than anything another person can do to us. Jesus' parable of the servant whose debt was forgiven by a king (debt— symbolic of the debt of sin we owe to God)— but who refused to forgive a minor debt of a friend. teaches us that if God's forgiveness toward us is limitless, so should ours be limitless toward others (Luke 17:3-4).

How Can I Help Those Struggling with Forgiveness?

People who have experienced abuse, trauma, or loss, need time to sort things out and let God bring them to the place of forgiveness in His time. God's timing is always the right time for each individual. The act of forgiving others is between God and us. The only time we need to forgive a person face-to-face is at the moment we are asked, by that person, to forgive them for the hurt they have caused.

There are things we can do to help those struggling with the forgiveness of others. We can support them with encouraging words and by listening to them. Taking our time and being gentle with them will allow them to progress through the steps of forgiveness the way God wants them to proceed.

Remember, every person will stand before God to be judged (Day of Judgment), "So then, each of us will give an account of himself to God" (Romans 14:12).

Notes: _____

_____

_____

_____

Give for the Joy of Giving - It All Belongs to God

Proverbs 3:9-10 (NKJV)

[9]Honor the Lord with your possessions and with the first fruits of all your increase; [10]so your barns will be filled with plenty, and your vats will overflow with new wine."

Luke 6:38 (NKJV)

[38]Give and it will be given to you: good measure, pressed down, shaken together, and running over will be put into your bosom. For with the same measure that you use, it will be measured back to you.

Proverbs 3:9 tells us to "Honor the Lord with your possessions and with the first fruits of your increase." When I would hear that Scripture being read, I use to think money, but possessions meant much more. It refers to everything we own, everything we have under our control.

I am hoping all of us will put a fresh perspective on this subject that usually causes people to squirm in their seats and avoid eye contact with pastors. **For a** fresh perspective on this subject, **take time to read Acts 27:9-10.** [9]"Now when much time had been spent, and sailing was now dangerous because the Fast was already over, Paul advised them, [10]Saying, 'Men, I perceive that this voyage will end with disaster and much loss, not only of the cargo and ship, but also our lives.'" Paul's warning was ignored, **and they went through a very rough time at sea in the midst of a storm.**

If we are to understand what it means to honor God with our possessions and with the first fruits of all our increase, **we must understand what Paul meant in Acts 27:23 when he said "God, whose I am, whom also I serve."**

Many Christians don't really understand what it means to really belong to God. To see yourself as belonging totally to God, you must put yourself in the place of those seamen in Acts 27 as they were going through that storm. You need to feel the salt spray on your cheek. You need to feel the ship rising and falling.

You need to hear the thunder of the waves against the bow of the ship. You need to see the flash of the lightning, feel the wind blowing against you so hard, that you can lean 45 degrees into it and not fall over. You are totally helpless. You have given up hope of ever seeing home again, of ever hugging your wife, your children, your grandchildren. You are going to die. Every possession you have, everything you hold dear, you would be willing to throw over the side of the ship if you could only feel dry ground under your feet again.

Nothing is as important as life at that moment. When you stare death in its face, everything of value fades away, except life.

Paul knew this. He knew that everything he was and ever would be, was totally tied up with Jesus Christ. He owed his very life to Jesus. In fact, Jesus was his LIFE.

Do you honor God with your possessions and first fruits? You may be asking yourself how you can honor God with material things that He does not need nor has any use for.

The answer is simple. Honor God with your possessions by supporting ministries and providing random acts of kindness to charities, organizations, and individuals. Volunteer where there is a need. God's blessings are His special gift, His charity in a sense. By giving to others with what God granted us, we enable others to share in the joy and love of God.

Leviticus 25:35-37 reads, [35]"If any of your fellow Israelites become poor and are unable to support themselves among you, help them as you would a foreigner and stranger, so they can continue to live among you." [36]"Do not take interest or any profit from them, but fear your God, so that they may continue to live among you." [37]"You must not lend them money at interest or sell them food at a profit."

Jesus summed up all the commandments as loving God and loving our neighbor. Honoring the Lord with our possessions/first fruits must be given out of love and appreciation. Give for the joy of giving because you realize that the people in need were created in the image of God who loves you, just as you were created. All are equal in the eyes of

God. "Walk in love, as Christ also has loved us and given Himself for us" (Ephesians 5:2).

Jesus has been referred to as God's first fruits given to us for our salvation (1 Corinthians 15:23). By following the example of Jesus and believing in our salvation, we become the first fruits of Jesus. James 1:18 reads, "Of His own will, He brought us forth by the word of truth, that we might be a kind of first fruits of His creatures." James does refer to spiritual fruit, but spiritual fruit is furthermore enacted in the world around us. "The fruit of the Spirit is love, joy, peace, longsuffering, kindness, goodness, gentleness, and self-control" (Galatians 5:22).

Sometimes, the words "love" and "charity" are interchangeable in the translations. Donate to those in need because of the love within your heart. Donate to ministries because through them, you obtain a deeper understanding and connection to God.

For generations, we have heard that all we need is faith for salvation. True enough, but what good is faith if we refuse to let it guide our actions, and if we deny spiritual fruits? Who docs our faith bcncfit?

"If a brother or sister is naked and destitute of daily food, and one of you says to them, 'Depart in peace, be warmed and filled,' but you do not give them the things which are needed for the body, what does it profit?" (James 2:15-16)

(James 2:18) "Show me your faith without your works, and I will show you my faith by my works."

Where is the love of Jesus within us if we never give our best?

If you find an individual in financial trouble circumstances, then you can provide clothing or money for other necessities. Donate to either local groups or large organizations that help people in need such as providing food, helping the homeless, or assisting families with medical troubles. Large organizations, that have a working ground force, are organizations which will use the money for the greater good.

If a particular ministry fills you with a love and understanding for God and for your neighbor, then you can donate to that ministry if it leads you and others to spiritual growth.

What better way is there to enable people to experience the love of God than by sharing that love with them?

I believe giving and offerings are made from a place of sacrifice. Abel brought his offering from a place of sacrifice. Abel gave his best to the Lord. Abel made a spiritual offering from a sacrifice. The blood offering represented something that cost him something, and that cost was beyond normal. Something had to die for something to live.

Sacrifice goes beyond normal giving; above what you usually give.

When you put God second, you give from a place of convenience. It is not a sacrifice to you, and it is not a sacrifice to God. That which is not a sacrifice to you will not be a sacrifice to God. **2 Samuel 24:24 reads, "I will not offer to God that which cost me nothing."**

A thankful heart will not come to God bearing a gift, which cost him nothing. If it is of no value to you, it will not be received nor blessed of God. So, give for the joy of giving. It all belongs to God.

Notes: _____

_____

_____

_____

_____

_____

_____

God-Centered

Psalm 1:1-6 (NKJV)

[1]Blessed is the man who walks not in the counsel of the ungodly, nor stands in the path of sinners, nor sits in the seat of the scornful; [2]But his delight is in the law of the LORD, and in His law he meditates day and night. [3]He shall be like a tree planted by the rivers of water, that brings forth its fruit in its season, whose leaf also shall not wither; And whatever he does shall prosper. [4]The ungodly are not so, but are like the chaff which the wind drives away. [5]Therefore the ungodly shall not stand in the judgment, nor sinners in the congregation of the righteous. [6]For the LORD knows the way of the righteous, but the way of the ungodly shall perish.

To be God-centered or focused is a phrase used to describe someone who puts God before everything, in everything they do. They honor God above all else and live their daily lives as ambassadors for him. 1 John 5:3-4: "This is love for God: to obey his commands. And his commands are not burdensome. For everyone born of God overcomes the world."

Those who live this way are "blessed." Have you ever asked persons how they're doing and the reply was, "I'm blessed," or "I'm blessed and highly favored?" I often wonder if they really mean that or if it's something that sounds good to them. I have also wondered if, when they are going through a storm, do they still feel blessed.

That frequent biblical word "blessed" contains more than what we call "happiness" in contemporary use. Our word "happy" has to do with "happenings." Something happens that makes us happy. The biblical concept of "blessedness" goes much deeper; it signifies a deep sense of joy based on your God-centered way of life. "Happiness" in modern use depends upon events or happenings; "blessedness" in biblical use is not influenced by events, but based on one's good relationship with God.

An illustration of this is when Jesus spoke to His disciples about the joy or blessedness they would have. In the same conversation He told them they would be hated and persecuted. "Blessed are you when men persecute you." The "man" or person of Psalms 1:1 possesses blessedness because his life is God-centered. There is a depth of comfort, satisfaction, and contentment he enjoys, regardless of the events of life, because His life doesn't depend upon events but upon His relationship with God.

He walks not in the counsel of the ungodly. Think about a child of God, staying close to his Father; walking with God, joining with others who walk with God. This child of God does not seek the counsel of the ungodly! This person gains motivation and guidance from his father, and good influence and association from his brothers and sisters. (Can you imagine attempting to gain self-improvement and spiritual stimulation by watching the Jerry Springer Show?)

He does not stand in the path of sinners. Apparently, the God-centered person is very careful about companionship. And, if you are walking in the pathway of righteousness (with God, toward heaven, following Christ), why would you stand in the path of sinners? The path of sinners moves in the opposite direction from your destination!

The God-centered person does not sit in the seat of the scornful. It is possible that the Holy Spirit is picturing for us a steady digression away from God and into sin. Walking, standing and then sitting may replicate that digression away from God. The point is the God-centered person doesn't do this.

The godly person avoids sin, stays on the right pathway, shuns the counsel of the ungodly, etc. In other words, this kind of person stays far away from sin and close to God. The result is that this person is blessed; biblical blessedness, not worldly happiness.

Are your thoughts, decisions, attitudes, and actions ordered by the Word of God, or do you take the advice of deceitful, wicked men? The person who lives a God-centered life "shall be like a tree planted in fertile, well-watered soil that brings forth fruit in its season!"

Of all of the doctrines of the Christian faith, the Trinity is perhaps the most confusing to outsiders. Many people of other faiths struggle to understand how Christians justify there being three persons, Father, Son, and Holy Spirit, who are all equally one God. Understanding the nature of this relationship requires an examination of many different Bible passages, which, when combined, form this important doctrine.

You may want to ask yourself, am I God-Centered or Self-Centered? Am I God Focused or Self-Focused?

Psalm 20:7 reads, "Some trust in chariots, and some in horses, but we trust in the name of the Lord our God."

In order to live a God-centered life, we must focus our lives on **God's purposes and ways**, and not our **own plans and schemes.**

We must seek to see things **from God's perspective**, not our own **incomplete and distorted** viewpoint.

1 Corinthians 13:12 reads, "For now we see in a mirror, **dimly**, but then face to face. Now I **know in part**, but then I shall know just as I also am known."

Living a God-centered life means that we must **deny ourselves** (i.e., our sinful nature) and seek only to do **God's Will.** Then God can accomplish **His purposes** through us, which will also yield **great blessings** as we **walk in the light** and **in the Spirit.**

Romans 8:28 reads, "And we know that all things work together for good to those who love God, to those who are called according to His purpose."

We are to keep our focus on God's will and purposes, not on our own needs/desires.

Matthew 6:33 reads, "But seek first the kingdom of God and His righteousness, and all these things shall be added to you."

We are to have confidence in God not self-reliance or worry.

"Therefore I say to you, do not worry about your life, what you will eat or what you will drink; nor about your body, what you will put on… For your heavenly Father knows that you need all these things." (Matthew 6:25, 32).

Our trust and dependence must be on God, not on self.

(Job 15:31) "Let him not trust in futile things, deceiving himself, for futility will be his reward."

We must deny self - stop obsessing about self-loss

(Matthew 16:24-26) [24]"If anyone desires to come after Me, let him deny himself, and take up his cross, and follow Me. [25]For whoever desires to save his life will lose it, but whoever loses his life for My sake will find it. [26]For what profit is it to a man if he gains the whole world, and loses his own soul? Or what will a man give in exchange for his soul?"

Jesus told us that we must **die to self** and **hate our life in this world** in order to **receive God's honor.** "Most assuredly, I say to you, unless a grain of wheat falls into the ground and dies, it remains alone."

In our fast-paced world, it is easy to get caught up in the daily grind and lose sight of our true purpose in life - the worship of God. Each believer, in striving to remain focused upon God, has his or her own way of keeping that focus. Each individual's needs are different. One person might memorize a Scripture verse each week; another might have a private Bible study each morning; yet another might have a goal of sharing the gospel message with at least one person every week. Each of these things keeps Christ at the forefront of one's mind.

Also, each of these activities has something in common. Each is something that believers can do in order to keep their focus where it needs to be. This is surrender-surrender to Jesus Christ, to God.

Surrendering one's whole life: needs, worries, pains, joys, praises. Surrendering the physical, the emotional, the mental, and the spiritual. Consider the following verses: Romans 12:1 (NLT): "And so, dear brothers and sisters, I plead with you to give your bodies to God. Let them be a living and holy sacrifice—the kind he will accept."

When you think of what he has done for you, is this too much to ask? Luke 9:23 reads, "Then he said to the crowd, 'If any of you wants to be my follower, you must put aside your selfish ambition, shoulder your cross daily, and follow me. If you try to keep your life for yourself, you will lose it. But if you give up your life for me, you will find true life.'"

Romans 6:13 reads, "Do not let any part of your body become a tool of wickedness, to be used for sinning. Instead, give yourselves completely to God since you have been given new life. And use your whole body as a tool to do what is right for the glory of God."

A surrendered life is all about trust. It is trusting that God has your best interests at heart. It is trusting that His Word can be believed and taken at face value. It is trusting that all your needs will be met. Surrender takes the focus off oneself and places it upon Christ and is demonstrated by obedience. Pastor Rick Warren of Saddleback Church in Lake Forest, California, writes, "Surrender is not the best way to live; it is the only way to live. Nothing else works. All other approaches lead to frustration, disappointment and self-destruction." I can't think of a better way to stay focused as a believer than to completely surrender our lives to our Lord and Savior.

Notes: _____

_____

_____

_____

_____

_____

God Gave His Son. What are You Willing to Give?

John 3:16 (NKJV)

[16]For God so loved the world that he gave his only begotten Son, so that everyone who believed in him shall not perish but have eternal life.

This is one, if not the most famous verse in the Bible. Believe it or not, it is also one of the verses people use to try to prove that Jesus is not God.

Simply put, without Jesus' death on the cross for our sins, no one would have eternal life. Jesus Himself said, (John 14:6) "I am the way and the truth and the life. No one comes to the Father except through me." In this statement, Jesus declares the reason for His birth, death, and resurrection—to provide the way to heaven for sinful mankind, who could never get there on their own.

The Father is the way God makes his decisions, the Holy Spirit is the way God inspires us to believe in him, and Jesus is the way God speaks to us. The title "Son of God," is a title Jesus used to describe his human birth, and a title he used to identify himself with the human race.

Also, it is his way of describing, or giving us an insight into the conversation that takes place in the mind of God between his distinct personalities. That is, they can tell each other apart, but they are not separate from each other.

People love quoting John 3:16. But who has truly sold out to the world to obtain this everlasting life that comes through believing in Jesus? It's more than quoting this verse, or even saying "I believe in Jesus." Jesus says, "if you love me, keep my commandments." In keeping His commandments, we must give up the world and follow Jesus.

We must deny self and take up the cross, giving up the pleasures and cares of this life that choke down the word of God. It's more than saying it; this is something we must do daily. God is not going to allow His only begotten Son to die in vain.

140

If we don't suffer with Him, we will not reign with Him. It's very important for us to realize that God wasn't making a mid-course change when he sent Jesus to us. Jesus was present at creation. That's why Genesis 1:26 says, Then God said, "Let us make man in our image, according to our likeness." The whole point of this verse is that the Father, Son, and Holy Spirit were all present when man was created. The same Triune God we worship today has been here since the beginning of time.

Now you may be thinking, if there is no doubt that God's plan was at work from the beginning, then why didn't he just go ahead and send Jesus to us instead of waiting for thousands of years?

Before God could send Jesus to save us, he gave us enough time to realize that we can't save ourselves from our own pride. The fact is, the Bible is full of stories about men and women who thought that they had control of their lives, only to realize that their destinies really depended upon the grace and mercy of God. From Adam to Paul, God's point is that man is sinful and his sinful nature will never change. Real hope can only come through redemption.

This is where Jesus comes in the picture. Because Jesus was fully God, his life was perfect and he enjoyed unqualified favor with God. That's exactly why God says immediately following Jesus' baptism, "This is my beloved son, in whom I am well pleased" (Matthew 3:17). Jesus is the exchange which redemption offers. God gives us the opportunity to trade our sins for his righteousness.

God also came to walk among us as a man because he desires a relationship with us. After all, you can't relate with someone, and they can't relate with you, if there aren't some common experiences.

More than anything else, we also need to understand that Jesus gave his life for us and for God. He took our sins all the way to the Cross so that we could take His cloak of righteousness all the way into eternity.

But what about God? Why did God give his only Son? You must understand Jesus didn't die so that we could go to heaven instead of hell. He died so that God could live, not in heaven, but in us.

The Apostle Paul says it another way, "Now he who establishes us with you in Christ and has anointed us is God, who also has sealed us and given us the spirit in our hearts as a guarantee" (2 Corinthians 1:21-22).

God sent his only begotten son to earth to make us sure about the existence of Himself. Jesus came from God and he witnessed his father in heaven. It means God exists and he is in a place called heaven. Jesus told us what God wants from us, and he showed it by self-demonstration.

He obeyed his father absolutely and therefore God raised him above all other names in the world. Absolute obedience to his father made him the Lord of this world. He is given authority to save anyone whom he wants. People who lived for God in this life, are also given glory by God, by making them saints.

All people do not become saints; but only those who have sacrificed their worldly life for the sake of God. Their names are also made great in this world, and generation after generation, everyone will know them, honor them, and pray through them.

Jesus' mission was to lead people from darkness to light, which he did. He also died for all those who would accept him as their personal savior. When a person believes in Jesus and obeys his commandments, he will receive salvation through Christ. God accepts Jesus' sacrifice on the cross as a compensation for our sins. But it needs our willful acceptance of Jesus as our Lord.

Because the wages of sin is death, all men have to pay for sin with death. The only way out and not to have to pay for your own sin, is to have someone stand in for you. Adam believed a lie and was reborn from life to death. For God to get his child back, he would have to send a scapegoat to pay that price. He would have to send a sinless man, one that could pay the price for another. One that didn't have to

142

pay for his own sinful nature. God does things to plant seeds and reap a harvest.

God sent one son and planted him in the earth. Jesus was raised up to become the firstborn of many brothers. From the book of Acts through the Revelation, Jesus is no longer referred to as God's only begotten son. But he is the firstborn from the dead. It is called the church of the firstborn. If there is a first, then there is a second. On the day of Pentecost there were 3000 sons and daughters born into that church.

I don't know what my number is, but I am born of the living God, raised from my sin and death nature, and am no longer a stranger from the covenants of promise. God's word is no longer strange to me. If you are in Christ, then are you Abraham's seed and heirs of the covenants of promise?

God is all-powerful, but he sent his only begotten Son to be in the form of man to die for our sins. Why did He send Jesus?

In the words of the song writer:

God sent His son, they called Him, Jesus; He came to love, heal and forgive; He lived and died to buy my pardon, An empty grave is there to prove our Savior lives! Because He lives, we can face tomorrow, Because He lives, all fear is gone; Because we know He holds the future, And life is worth the living, Just because He lives!

No matter what we are going through, no matter what situation we find ourselves in, not some, but all fear is gone. Why did He send Jesus? He sent Jesus because He loves us.

"For God so loved the world, that He gave His only begotten Son, that whoever believes in Him shall not perish, but have eternal life" (John 3:16). Everyone wants to be loved. But sometimes, love is given only if it is earned. It wasn't like that with God. He loved us when we didn't deserve it. "God demonstrates His own love toward us, in that while we were yet sinners, Christ died for us" (Romans 5:8).

Where love has been sought ... none was found. However, we don't have to feel that way. We are loved ... God loves us. Motivated by love, God sent Jesus to provide the gift of eternal life, and that eternal life is more than living forever.

The Bible makes it clear that everyone will live forever; no one will be extinguished. What is God's gift of eternal life? Jesus defined it as, "This is eternal life, that they may know You, the only true God, and Jesus Christ whom You have sent" (John 17: 3).

His gift of eternal life is a personal relationship with Him – one that continues into eternity.

May God bless you and keep you is my prayer. Amen.

Notes: _____

_____

_____

_____

_____

_____

_____

_____

_____

_____

_____

_____

_____

_____

God Is Glorified When We Pray for Others

Ephesians 6:18 (NKJV)

[18]Praying always with all prayer and supplication in the Spirit, being watchful to this end with all perseverance and supplication for all the saints.

Philippians 4:6-7 (NKJV)

[6]Be anxious for nothing, but in everything by prayer and supplication, with thanksgiving, let your requests be made known to God; [7] and the peace of God, which surpasses all understanding, will guard your hearts and minds through Christ Jesus.

Why Prayer? Why Now?

I love praying for others. I love hearing testimonies of how God Has blessed and healed those who we are praying for. While reading the book *Beyond All You Could Ask or Think* by Ray Prichard, I realized God is being greatly glorified when we pray for others. I'd never thought about it before. Many Christians enjoy praying for others, but it wasn't until I read this book that I realized we glorify God when we pray for others because we are responding to others needs in a Christlike manner. We are demonstrating that we believe God's word about prayer is true. We are one part of the body of Christ, moving to meet the needs of another part, and we are partnering with God to further His work in the world. God gets all the glory when the answer comes.

Sometimes we may look at intercessory prayer as a burden or a distraction from the real work of life. But nothing could be further from the truth. God is greatly pleased when we pray for others.

Through intercessory prayer we partner with God in helping those in need. The idea of partnering with God is an exciting concept. It means when we are praying, we make contact with the most powerful force in the universe.

I'm encouraging everyone to pray for one another. When we pray, we are in touch with Almighty God himself, the Creator of heaven and earth. It doesn't matter if you don't know what's going on in someone's life. The Holy Spirit aids us in linking up with the heart of God when we do not know what to pray.

Romans 8:26-27 reads, [26]"Likewise the Spirit also helps in our weaknesses. For we do not know what we should pray for as we ought, but the Spirit Himself makes intercession for us with groanings which cannot be uttered. [27]Now He who searches the hearts knows what the mind of the Spirit *is,* because He makes intercession for the saints according to the will of God."

By prayer we are knocking holes in the darkness and rolling back Satan's evil dominion. That's why the devil trembles when he sees the weakest saint on his knees.

In closing, we know there's power in prayer. But there is even more power when we come together to pray and everyone is in agreement with what we are praying for.

"One can put a thousand to flight, but two can put ten thousand to flight" (Deuteronomy 32:30). Applying this principle to prayer, we could say that every time you add one person to the group who is in agreement with what you're praying for, and is standing in faith for the answer, the effectiveness of the group against the enemy increases 10 times.

There are at least two things that happen when we pray together that cannot happen when we pray alone. First, when we pray together, our faith is strengthened. If we are in a small group, it is inevitable that some people will come with strong faith, others with weak faith and others somewhere in-between.

As we pray, the prayer of one person will speak something to another person and vice versa, and we all leave the prayer time with stronger faith than we had in the beginning.

Second, when we pray together, the joy is multiplied when the answer finally comes. We've seen it happen, I'm sure. I can't speak for anyone else, but I know when someone asks me to pray for them and they come back with a praise report that the prayer was answered, I'm excited. Who knows, it could have been my prayer God heard that day that blessed them. Again, I'm asking all of us to pray for one another and encourage one another. Prayer and encouragement will lift the spirit of others.

May God continue to bless you and keep you is my prayer. Amen.

Notes: _____

_____

_____

_____

_____

_____

_____

_____

_____

_____

_____

_____

_____

_____

_____

_____

_____

Have Faith in God

Psalm 30:5 (NLT)

⁵For his anger lasts only a moment, but his favor lasts a lifetime! Weeping may last through the night, but joy comes with the morning.

Psalm 55:22 (NKJV)

Cast your burden on the LORD, And He shall sustain you; He shall never permit the righteous to be moved.

Weeping may endure for a night, but joy comes with the morning, is a verse from the bible, that I have heard most of my life. For the longest time I had no idea what that meant. Some of the struggles I was going through when those words were spoken to me were still there the next morning. Finally, I realized that Scripture simply means you might have to cry for a while, but when you're through crying, there will be much joy.

Anyone can have faith in God during fair weather; but, the true TEST of our faith is how we respond during stormy weather, when we can't see our hand in front of our face. I have heard people say it's not how you go through the storm; it's how you dance in the rain. Most Christians have a very weak faith, a shallow faith, and a temporary faith; which means when the winds of a violent storm arise, they quit and behave no better than the unbelievers.

Christ should be our example during our times of pain, mental anguish, and suffering. I'm sure some of us know the overwhelming feeling of mental anguish. I've heard people say there have been times in their lives when they wished they'd never been born. When I hear someone say that, I will share with them what God promised in Psalm 30:5, that "weeping only endureth for a night, but joy cometh in the morning."

Perhaps you feel that nothing you could ever do would make things right in your life. May I say to you, that is why Jesus came into the world, to make things right, because we cannot. Jesus came to make everything right through His blood sacrifice. Thanks be to God, Jesus has paid our sin debt, to set us free from the enslavement of sin (John 8:32-36). Jesus Christ has set the believer free from the curse of the law. Amen!

I'm sure some of us know what it's like to suffer overwhelming, emotional pain. Some of us probably know what it's like to wake up from a nightmare to a bigger nightmare, unable to do anything about the situation. There have been many times in my life, when every second seemed like an hour, and every hour like a day, and every day like a never-ending eternity. At those times, the only friend I had in the world was Jesus.

I am often reminded of the words in the song, "What a Friend We Have in Jesus:"

What a friend we have in Jesus:

Oh what peace we often forfeit,

Oh what needless pain we bear,

because we do not take it to the Lord in prayer.

John 16:33 (NLT): "I have told you all this so that you may have peace in me. Here on Earth you will have many trials and sorrows. But take heart, because I have overcome the world."

Psalm 55:22: "Cast your burden on the LORD, And He shall sustain you; He shall never permit the righteous to be moved."

Whenever we are burdened, God promises to sustain us and not let us be moved (or shaken).

But there is something we must do to receive this promise. We must cast our burdens on the Lord.

We often talk about casting our burdens on the Lord. But what does that really mean?

I believe it means, first we must turn to God through Jesus - Don't just say "it will be fine," or "it will all work out," or "God will take care of it."

None of those involve you actually meeting with the Living God, so turn your heart to God Himself. Come to God, cleansed by Christ's blood and clothed with His righteousness.

Turn to God and know that through Christ he loves you, welcomes you, and promises to help you. Hebrews 4:16 (NLT) tells us to come boldly to the throne of our gracious God. There we will receive his mercy, and we will find grace to help us when we need it most.

Second, ask God to keep this painful event from happening.

Ask God to save your marriage, keep you employed, save your children, give you good health.

To strengthen your faith, think about times when God delivered His people — Israel from Egypt, Joseph from his dungeon, Bartimaeus from his blindness.

Strengthen your faith, then pray that God would deliver you from this painful event. Psalm 50:15 (NKJV) says: "Call upon Me in the day of trouble; I will deliver you, and you shall glorify me."

God may choose to deliver you, which would be a great mercy. But the Bible also teaches that He may not, which is why at this point you probably still feel burdened. Therefore, this next step is so crucial.

Third, trust that if He allows this painful event to happen, it's to bring you more joy in Him.

Your greatest joy is knowing God, beholding God, loving God. Psalm 16:11 says: "You will show me the path of life; In Your presence *is* fullness of joy; at Your right hand are pleasures forevermore." And God promises to orchestrate everything — including every pain, sorrow, and trial — to bring you even more joy in Him. Romans 8:18 says: "For I consider that the sufferings of this present time are not worthy *to* be compared with the glory which shall be revealed in us."

Take time to set your heart on God. Use His Word to help you see His love, majesty, glory, and grace. Pray over God's Word until the Holy Spirit helps you see and feel the all-surpassing worth of God, the Father, and Jesus, the Son.

Now, look at your future. You see that this painful event might happen. But now you also see that if it does, it will mean not just pain, but gain. The gain of more joy in God now and forever.

Finally, trust that if God allows this painful event to happen, He will take care of every need it creates.

He will. He promises. He will provide:

- All the wisdom you need to make tough decisions. (James 1:5): "If any of you lacks wisdom, let him ask of God, who gives to all liberally and without reproach, and it will be given to him."

- All the finances you need to fulfill His call on your life. (Matt 6:33) "But seek first the kingdom of God and His righteousness, and all these things shall be added to you."

- All the comfort you need for your heartaches. (2 Corinthians 1:3-4) "Blessed be the God and Father of our Lord Jesus Christ, the Father of mercies and God of all comfort, [4] who comforts us in all our tribulation, that we may be able to comfort those who are in any trouble, with the comfort with which we ourselves are comforted by God."

- All the grace you need to keep faithful to Him. (2 Corinthians 9:8) "And God is able to make all grace abound toward you, that you, always having all sufficiency in all things, may have an abundance for every good work."

- All the strength you need to persevere. (Philippians 4:13) "I can do all things through Christ who strengthens me."

- All the joy in Him you need to make this all worth it. (Romans 8:18) "For I consider that the sufferings of this present time are not worthy to be compared with the glory which shall be revealed in us."

Pray over these promises until the Holy Spirit strengthens your faith. Pray until you trust that God will take care of your every need.

Cast your burden on the LORD, and He shall sustain you (Psalm 55:22).

Notes: _____

_____

_____

_____

_____

_____

_____

_____

_____

_____

_____

_____

_____

_____

_____

_____

_____

_____

_____

_____

_____

Having the Mind of Jesus

Philippians 2:3-11 (NLT)

³Let nothing be done through selfish ambition or conceit, but in lowliness of mind let each esteem others better than himself. ⁴Let each of you look out not only for his own interests, but also for the interests of others. ⁵Let this mind be in you which was also in Christ Jesus, ⁶who, being in the form of God, did not consider it robbery to be equal with God, ⁷but made Himself of no reputation, taking the form of a bondservant, and coming in the likeness of men. ⁸And being found in appearance as a man, He humbled Himself and became obedient to the point of death, even the death of the cross. ⁹Therefore God also has highly exalted Him and given Him the name which is above every name, ¹⁰that at the name of Jesus every knee should bow, of those in heaven, and of those on earth, and of those under the earth, ¹¹and that every tongue should confess that Jesus Christ is Lord, to the glory of God the Father.

Many people, even Christians, live only to make a good impression on others or to please themselves. But "selfish ambition, or vain conceit" brings discord. Paul, therefore, stressed spiritual unity, asking the Philippians to love one another and to be one in spirit and purpose.

When we work together, caring for the problems of others as if they were our problems, we demonstrate Christ's example of putting others first, and we experience unity. We should offer a helping hand whenever we can. There are many persons who need help but won't ask for it. We can't be so concerned about making a good impression or meeting our own needs that we strain relationships in God's family.

The Bible has a lot to say about rewards and recognition. As Christians in the marketplace, we have an advantage over our co-workers who are non-believers, because we work for a higher level of management than they do, and our manager has a wonderful program of recognition and reward.

In Colossians 3:23 we read: "Whatever you do, work at it with all your heart, as working for the Lord, not for men, since you know that you will receive an inheritance from the Lord as a reward. It is the Lord Christ you are serving."

Verse 3

Selfish ambition can ruin a church, but genuine humility can build it. Being humble involves having a true perspective about ourselves. Romans 12:3: "Because of the privilege and authority God has given me, I give each of you this warning: Don't think you are better than you really are. Be honest in your evaluation of yourselves, measuring yourselves by the faith God has given us." This does not mean that we should put ourselves down. Before God, we are all sinners, saved only by God's grace, but we are saved and therefore have great worth in God's kingdom. We are to lay aside selfishness and treat others with respect and common courtesy. Considering others' interests as more important than our own links us with Christ, who was a true example of humility.

Verse 4

Philippi was a cosmopolitan city. The composition of the church reflected great diversity, with people from a variety of backgrounds and walks of life. Acts 16 gives us some indication of the diverse makeup of this church. It's likely that, with so many different backgrounds among the members, unity must have been difficult to maintain. Although there is no evidence of division in the church, its unity had to be safeguarded (Philippians 3:2; Philippians 4:2). Paul encourages us to guard against any selfishness, prejudice, or jealousy that might lead to dissension. Showing genuine interest in others is a positive step forward in maintaining unity among believers.

Verse 5

Jesus Christ was humble, willing to give up his rights in order to obey God and serve people. Like Christ, we should have a servant's attitude, serving out of love for God and for others, not out of guilt or fear. Remember, you can choose your own attitude. You can approach life expecting to be served, or you can look for opportunities to serve others. Mark 10:45: "For even the Son of Man did not come to be served, but to serve, and to give His life a ransom for many."

Philippians 2:5-7: "Without ceasing to be God, He became a human being, the man called Jesus. He did not give up his deity to become human, but he set aside the right to his glory and power." In submission to the Father's will, Christ limited his power and knowledge. Jesus of Nazareth was subject to place, time, and many other human limitations. What made his humanity unique was his freedom from sin. In his full humanity, Jesus showed us everything about God's character that can be conveyed in human terms.

Philippians 2:5-11: Here are some of the key characteristics of Jesus Christ, praised in the passage of Scripture read earlier: (1) Jesus has always existed with God; (2) Jesus is equal to God because he is God (John 1:1; Colossians 1:15-19); (3) though Jesus is God, he became a man in order to fulfill God's plan of salvation for all people; (4) Jesus did not just have the appearance of being a man -- he actually became human to identify with our sins; (5) Jesus voluntarily laid aside his divine rights and privileges out of love for his Father; (6) Jesus died on the cross for our sins so we wouldn't have to face eternal death; (7) God glorified Jesus because of his obedience; (8) God raised Jesus to his original position at the Father's right hand, where he will reign forever as our Lord and Judge. *There is nothing better than knowing Jesus. He will pick you up and turn your life around. There is nothing better than knowing Jesus. He gets sweeter as the days go by.*

How can we do anything less than praise Jesus as our Lord and dedicate ourselves to his service!

Often people excuse selfishness, pride, or evil by claiming their rights and do what's convenient for them. They think, "I can cheat on this test; after all, I deserve to pass this class," or "I can spend all this money on myself -- I worked hard for it," or "I can get an abortion; I have a right to control my own body." But as believers, we should have a different attitude, one that enables us to lay aside our rights in order to serve others. If we say we follow Christ, we must also say we

155

want to live as he lived. We should develop his attitude of humility as we serve, even when we are not likely to get recognition for our efforts. Are you selfishly clinging to your rights, or are you willing to serve?

Jesus died on a cross for our sins. Death on a cross (crucifixion) was the form of capital punishment that Romans used for notorious criminals. It was excruciatingly painful, and humiliating. Prisoners were nailed or tied to a cross and left to die. Death might not come for several days, and it usually came by suffocation when the weight of the weakened body made breathing more and more difficult. Jesus died as one who was cursed. (Galatians 3:13): "Christ has redeemed us from the curse of the law, having become a curse for us (for it is written, "Cursed is everyone who hangs on a tree."" How amazing, that the perfect man should die this most shameful death, so that we would not have to face eternal punishment!

Verses 9-11

At the last judgment, even those who are condemned will recognize Jesus' authority and right to rule.

Let's briefly compare earthly rewards with heavenly rewards. If you're working for man's recognition, be prepared to discover that it is not fairly given. Some people get recognition they don't deserve and some who deserve it, never get it. Also, you'll notice that earthly recognition is unreliable: one day you have it, the next day it's gone. Furthermore, earthly rewards don't last very long. The money goes fast, the kudos are quickly forgotten, the bigger office and title soon lose their attraction. As hard as we may work to get earthly recognition and rewards, we will always find them to be less-than-satisfying.

However, God's rewards are eternal. Colossians 3:24-25: "Remember that the Lord will give you an inheritance as your reward, and that the Master you are serving is Christ. [25]But if you do what is wrong, you will be paid back for the wrong you have done. For God has no favorites." If we do right, we have the potential to hear Jesus Christ say to us, "Well done, good and faithful servant." God's recognition will last through eternity; it will be fairly distributed, so you can be assured that if you deserve it, you will receive it.

And so, in honor of the name of Jesus, all beings in heaven, on earth, and in the world below will fall on their knees.

People can choose to regard Jesus as Lord now, as a step of willing and loving commitment, or be forced to acknowledge him as Lord when he returns. Jesus Christ may return at any moment. Are you prepared to meet him?

Notes: _____

_____

_____

_____

_____

_____

_____

_____

_____

_____

_____

_____

_____

_____

Humble Me Lord, and Let Me Do Thy Will

Luke 18:9-14 (NIV)

[9] To some who were confident of their own righteousness and looked down on everyone else, Jesus told this parable: [10] Two men went up to the temple to pray, one a Pharisee and the other a tax collector. [11] The Pharisee stood by himself and prayed: 'God, I thank you that I am not like other people—robbers, evildoers, adulterers—or even like this tax collector. [12] I fast twice a week and give a tenth of all I get.' [13] But the tax collector stood at a distance. He would not even look up to heaven, but beat his breast and said, 'God, have mercy on me, a sinner.' [14] I tell you that this man, rather than the other, went home justified before God. For all those who exalt themselves will be humbled, and those who humble themselves will be exalted.

Being humble means not being proud, not thinking of yourself as being more important than other people. The Bible has so much to say about being humble. Maybe we've got it all wrong and the one who practices humility is actually the strong one.

1 Peter 5:6-7: "Humble yourselves, therefore, under the mighty hand of God so that at the proper time He may exalt you, casting all your anxieties on Him, because He cares for you."

God cares for us. God is mighty. God calls us to humble ourselves under Him, not because He is a controlling God that wants you to bow down to Him because you are nothing, but rather because God wants to exalt us and care for us. As we humble ourselves, that's when we truly worship God. We're trusting God with what's going on in our lives and believing He is the provider instead of ourselves.

We should stop putting everything on our shoulders. We get so tired. We're busy. We're weary. We don't feel good. We take on a lot of responsibilities. We're working hard for our families. We're trying to attend social events. We're trying to pay the bills as best as we can. We're just trying to "get by."

Matthew 11:28-30: "Come to me, all who labor and are heavy laden, and I will give you rest. Take my yoke upon you, and learn from me, for I am gentle and lowly in heart, and you will find rest for your souls. For my yoke is easy, and my burden is light."

Jesus doesn't seem to be talking about a life that is full of anxiousness and weariness as we follow Him. He makes a point of stating the exact opposite on how we can find rest in Him. He is speaking to those that labor and are heavy laden.

I can't speak for anyone else, but I remember not so long ago, I use to suffer from this. I was working too hard. I was thinking way too much. The bottom line is, I was putting things on my shoulders that didn't belong there. I think a lot of us forget what Jesus said and what He has done when we feel that it's "all on us" to make things happen. Most of the time, we're probably putting too much effort into the wrong things. (I am guilty of this, too, but I'm getting better.)

In today's culture, we're told if you labor and are heavy laden, then you are doing the right thing. You are sacrificing for your family and friends. You arc pulling yourself up by your bootstraps and working hard to hopefully, one day, achieve paradise (retirement) where you get to do nothing as you live out the rest of your days. This is wrong. Don't let culture tell you that putting everything on your shoulders is wisdom. Trust Jesus when He tells you that His burden is light.

Philippians 4:4-8: "Rejoice in the Lord always; again I will say, Rejoice. Let your reasonableness be known to everyone. The Lord is at hand; do not be anxious about anything, but in everything by prayer and supplication with thanksgiving let your requests be made known to God. And the peace of God, which surpasses all understanding, will guard your hearts and your minds in Christ Jesus. Finally, brothers, whatever is true, whatever is honorable, whatever is just, whatever is pure, whatever is lovely, whatever is commendable, if there is any excellence, if there is anything worthy of praise, think about these things."

Most of the time when we don't humble ourselves, we are really saying we don't trust God. There are times as a follower of Christ

159

when we forget God's character or doubt Him. We're told in Scripture to think on the things of God, to meditate on anything worthy of praise.

These things that are true, honorable, just, pure, lovely, commendable, or excellent are all praiseworthy because God is all these things. You'll never find an area of the Bible that contradicts God's character at the end of the day and that should encourage us in those moments of doubt. When we don't humble ourselves, we are really saying we don't trust God. Most of all, when God gave His one and only Son for us (John 3:16), it tells us a lot about His character.

God knew that we could only come to Him through His Son who had to suffer and die before rising again. With that perfect knowledge that only God has, He followed through and sacrificed His Son for us. Not only does that tell us everything we need to know about God's character, that shows us just how much He loves us.

Jesus is our ultimate example of humility.

Philippians 2:8-11: "And being found in human form, He humbled Himself by becoming obedient to the point of death, even death on a cross. Therefore, God has highly exalted Him and bestowed on Him the name that is above every name, so that at the name of Jesus, every knee should bow, in heaven and on earth and under the earth, and every tongue confess that Jesus Christ is Lord, to the glory of God the Father."

If Jesus practiced humility Himself, then why would we think we don't need to? Why would we consider this a weakness? Even Jesus was dependent on His Father and this was a good thing, in fact, the best thing. It was a God glorifying thing in every way. We couldn't even have a relationship with God if it wasn't for what Jesus did for us in the first place (John 14:6). We had to humble ourselves to trust that Jesus is King and to ask Him to be our Lord and Savior. This is no different today whether you've been a believer for a week or fifty years. We still need Him in everything we do.

We still need the Holy Spirit to guide us and give us wisdom in all matters. We still need help to practice things that are honorable, pure, lovely, commendable, and anything praiseworthy. We are still not capable of doing anything on our own and will never be. As soon as we begin to live in a way where we are no longer dependent on God to do everything for us, we are forgetting our first love and proclaiming what Christ did for us was not enough.

As a follower of Christ, no matter what circumstance you find yourself in, I promise that you can give it to Him. This is because God's Word is true. What Jesus did *was* enough.

When you humble yourself to Jesus you are saying:

Have Thine own way, Lord! Have Thine own way!
Thou art the Potter, I am the clay.
Mold me and make me after Thy will,
While I am waiting, yielded and still.

Have Thine own way, Lord! Have Thine own way!
Search me and try me, Master, today!
Whiter than snow, Lord, wash me just now;
As in Thy presence humbly I bow.

My brothers and sisters I thank God that we have the Holy Spirit and we can trust Him to lead and guide us. So, humble yourself and pray to God, truly casting your anxieties to the Lord, knowing He cares for you.

Since the Father attaches such great importance to being humble, what can we all do to be in line with His will? Think about it. May God bless you and keep you always, is my prayer, in Jesus' name, Amen.

Notes: _____

_____

_____

_____

_____

_____

_____

_____

_____

_____

_____

_____

_____

_____

_____

_____

_____

_____

_____

_____

_____

I Am Redeemed

Psalm 107: 2-9 (KJV)

2Let the redeemed of the LORD say so, whom he hath redeemed from the hand of the enemy; 3And gathered them out of the lands, from the east, and from the west, from the north, and from the south. 4They wandered in the wilderness in a solitary way; they found no city to dwell in. 5Hungry and thirsty, their soul fainted in them. 6Then they cried unto the LORD in their trouble, and he delivered them out of their distresses. 7And he led them forth by the right way that they might go to a city of habitation. 8Oh, that men would praise the LORD for his goodness, and for his wonderful works to the children of men! 9For he satisfieth the longing soul and filleth the hungry soul with goodness."

Redemption is a biblical word that means "a purchase" or "a ransom." Historically, redemption was used in reference to the purchase of a slave's freedom. A slave was "redeemed" when the price was paid for his freedom. God spoke of Israel's deliverance from slavery in Egypt in this way:

Exodus 6:6: "I am the LORD, and I will bring you out from under the burdens of the Egyptians, and I will deliver you from slavery to them, and I will redeem you with an outstretched arm and with great acts of judgment." The use of redemption in the New Testament includes this same idea. Every person is a slave to sin; only through the price Jesus paid on the cross is a sinful person redeemed from sin and death.

In Scripture, it is clear every person stands in need of redemption. Why? Because every person has sinned (Romans 3:23). The following verse then reveals we are "justified by his grace as a gift, through the redemption that is in Christ Jesus" (Romans 3:24). Hebrews 9:15: Jesus "is the mediator of a new covenant, since a death has occurred that redeems them from the transgressions committed under the first covenant."

When we are redeemed, we become different people. When God redeemed Israel from slavery in Egypt, He made them a new nation and gave them a new land. Likewise, the Christian has a new identity in Christ. No longer is the Christian a captive to sin and death. Instead, he has become a citizen of God's kingdom. Christians now live in anticipation of our eternal home with our heavenly Father.

Everyone needs redemption. Our natural condition was characterized by guilt: "all have sinned and fallen short of the glory of God" (Romans 3:23). Christ's redemption has freed us from guilt, being "justified freely by His grace through the redemption that is in Christ Jesus" (Romans 3:24). The benefits of redemption include eternal life (Revelation 5:9-10), forgiveness of sins (Ephesians 1:7), righteousness (Romans 5:17), freedom from the law's curse (Galatians 3:13), adoption into God's family (Galatians 4:5), deliverance from sin's bondage (Titus 2:14; 1 Peter 1:14-18), peace with God (Colossians 1:18-20), and the indwelling of the Holy Spirit (1 Corinthians 6:19-20). To be redeemed, then, is to be forgiven, holy, justified, free, adopted, and reconciled.

The word redeem means: "to buy out." The term was used specifically in reference to the purchase of a slave's freedom. The application of this term to Christ's death on the cross is quite telling. If we are "redeemed," then our prior condition was one of slavery. God has purchased our freedom, and we are no longer in bondage to sin or to the Old Testament law. This metaphorical use of "redemption" is the teaching of Galatians 3:13 and 4:5. Related to the Christian concept of redemption is the word ransom. Jesus paid the price for our release from sin and its consequences (Matthew 20:28; 1 Timothy 2:6). His death was in exchange for our life. In fact, Scripture is quite clear that redemption is only possible "through His blood," that is, by His death.

The streets of heaven will be filled with former captives who, through no merit of their own, find themselves redeemed, forgiven, and free. Slaves to sin have become saints. No wonder we will sing a new song—a song of praise to the Redeemer who was slain (Revelation 5:9).

We were slaves to sin, condemned to eternal separation from God. Jesus paid the price to redeem us, resulting in our freedom from slavery to sin and our rescue from the eternal consequences of that sin.

Can I pause right here for a public announcement to share with you, that this is A Costly Redemption and not one of us can really estimate what price Jesus paid for redeeming us? We know that Jesus suffered excruciatingly at Calvary. In fact, the very word "excruciating" comes from the root word crucifixion. We should also understand that the Father suffered in this redemption too, because He had to endure the suffering of His One and Only Unique Son, Jesus Christ.

We often only think about what Jesus suffered but if you are a parent, can you imagine the suffering that the Father must have endured as well? Surely this was also tremendously painful for the Father. Peter writes that "because Christ also suffered for you, leaving you an example, so that you might follow in his steps" (1 Peter 2:21) and "When he was spoken about in an insulting way he did not insult in return; when he suffered, he did not threaten, but continued entrusting himself to him who judges justly. He himself bore our sins in his body on the tree, that we might die to sin and live to righteousness. By his wounds you have been healed" (1 Peter 2:23-24).

My question for you is, have you been redeemed by the blood of the Lamb of God? If not, you still have the wrath of God abiding on you (John 3:36b). Today, if you will hear the voice of the Holy Spirit, don't reject this appeal again, because your heart will become hardened even more every time you reject His call (2 Corinthians 6:2). You will someday reach a point where you can no longer hear His voice and the ultimate decision of yours to reject Him will result in an eternal separation from God (Rev 20:12-15). There is still time, before He returns, to claim Him as your only way to be saved (Acts 4:12) and call Him your Savior, otherwise He will be your Judge. *Jesus paid it all, all to Him I owe. Sin has left a crimson stain, but Jesus washed us white as snow. I know Jesus Christ paid the price for me.* I can say today, in the words of the songwriter:

I Am Redeemed.

I am Redeemed, bought with a price
Jesus has changed my whole life
If anybody asks you just who I am
I'll tell them, I am redeemed!
Where there was hate, love now abides
Where there was confusion, peace now reigns
I'm walking with Jesus, I'm a child of the King
It's all because I am redeemed

So, I'll tell of His favor, I'll tell of His love
I'll tell of His goodness to me
He purchased my redemption with His own precious blood
And from sin, I've been set free.

So, "Let the redeemed of the LORD say so."

Notes: _____

_____

_____

_____

_____

_____

_____

_____

_____

_____

_____

In All Things Give Thanks

Psalm 92:1-2 (NKJV)

[1]It is good to give thanks to the LORD, And to sing praises to Your name, O Most High; [2]To declare Your loving kindness in the morning, And Your faithfulness every night.

We are quick to make our requests and slow to thank God for His answers. Because God so often answers our prayers, we come to expect it. We forget that it is only by His grace that we receive anything from Him. The Bible repeatedly stresses the importance of giving thanks.

As a matter of fact, the Bible is filled with commands to give thanks to God (Psalm 106:1; 107:1; 118:1; 1 Chronicles 16:34; 1 Thessalonians 5:18). Most verses go on to list reasons why we should thank Him, such as "His love endures forever" (Psalm 136:3), "He is good" (Psalm 118:29), and "His mercy is everlasting" (Psalm 100:5). Thanksgiving and praise always go together. We cannot adequately praise and worship God, without also being thankful.

When we make a practice of thanking God for His many blessings, we will be focusing on the good things He has given us, and He can begin to bring healing and strength to us. Our Lord knew the importance of giving thanks. Before feeding the five thousand, Jesus "took the loaves; and having given thanks, He distributed to those who were seated."

For me, every day is a day of thanksgiving. In the stressful and troubled world in which we live, if we don't have a relationship with God, it can seem difficult to find something to be thankful for. When we listen to or read the news, it is mostly bad news that is reported.

We hear of crime, terrorism, tragedies, and disasters. We rush about at a hectic pace day after day, trying to keep up with the demands of modern life. And the list of problems could go on and on. Yet, it is precisely because of the problems around us that we need to devote ourselves to giving thanks. 1 Thessalonians 5: 16-18, (NRSV):

"...[18]Give thanks in all circumstances; for this is the will of God in Christ Jesus for you."

Joy can be the constant experience of the Christian, even in the most adverse circumstances, because Christ is the subject and source of his joy and Christ is in control of the circumstances. **"Rejoice Always"** is the shortest verse in the Greek NT, even if "Jesus Wept" is the shortest in the English translation.

Giving thanks to God should be Christian native emotion. Romans 8:28 says, "And we know that all things work together for good to those who love God, to those who are the called according to His purpose." If this is true, we should be able to praise the Lord at all times and in all circumstances and for everything, just as long as in doing so we do not excuse sin.

When darkness grows around us, we cannot afford to become neglectful in this spiritual practice. Instead, we need to renew our commitment to thankfulness. If you were asked what you're most thankful for, what would you say? Many people start with being thankful for life, relationships, children, and/or jobs.

But what can believers be thankful for when persecution threatens life, marriages break up, children become prodigals, unemployment looms, or food becomes rationed? If you are a believer in the Lord Jesus Christ, you can be thankful even in times of distress no matter who you are, where you live, or what you do in life. (Ephesians 5:20, NIV): "Always giving thanks to God the Father for everything, in the name of our Lord Jesus Christ." There are many things we can be thankful for.

Feeling and expressing appreciation is good for us. Like any wise father, God wants us to learn to be thankful for all the gifts He has given us (James 1:17). It is in our best interest to be reminded that everything we have is a gift from Him. Without gratefulness, we become arrogant and self-centered. We begin to believe that we have achieved everything on our own. Thankfulness keeps our hearts in right relationship to the Giver of all good gifts.

Giving thanks also reminds us of how much we do have. Human beings are prone to covetousness. We tend to focus on what we don't have. By giving thanks continually, we are reminded of how much we do have. When we focus on blessings rather than wants, we are happier. When we start thanking God for the things we usually take for granted, our perspective changes. We realize that we could not even exist without the merciful blessings of God.

1 Thessalonians 5:18: "In everything give thanks; for this is God's will for you in Christ Jesus." We are to be thankful, not only for the things we like, but for the circumstances we don't like. When we thank God for everything that He allows to come into our lives, we keep bitterness at bay.

We cannot be both thankful and bitter at the same time. We do not thank Him for evil, but that He is sustaining us through it (James 1:12). We don't thank Him for harm He did not cause, but we thank Him when He gives us the strength to endure it (2 Corinthians 12:9). We thank Him for His promise that "all things will work together for the good, to those who love God and are called according to His purpose" (Romans 8:28).

We can have thankful hearts toward God, even when we do not feel thankful for the circumstance. We can grieve and still be thankful. We can hurt and still be thankful. We can be angry at sin and still be thankful toward God. That is what the Bible calls a "sacrifice of praise" (Hebrews 13:15). Giving thanks to God keeps our hearts in right relationship with Him and saves us from a host of harmful emotions and attitudes that will rob us of the peace God wants us to experience (Philippians 4:6–7).

Give thanks today!

What should make Christians most thankful is the work of Christ. So, when we are in a season of suffering, it may be difficult to be thankful. During those times, be thankful for the work of Christ, which is our salvation.

169

By the grace of God, your eyes can be opened to always find something to thank Him for. Sometimes it's easier to focus on what we don't have, rather than what we do have. It's important to take time out and remember all the things to be thankful for that many of us take for granted. Always be thankful to God in all circumstances for all His blessings. May God continue to bless you and keep you is my prayer.

Notes: _____

_____

_____

_____

_____

_____

_____

_____

_____

_____

_____

_____

_____

_____

_____

_____

_____

Is Your Faith Moving You to Prepare for the Future?

Hebrews 11:7 (NRSV)

[7]By faith, Noah, warned by God about events as yet unseen, respected the warning and built an ark to save his household; by this he condemned the world and became an heir to the righteousness that is in accordance with faith.

There are numerous stories in the Bible about faith being tested: Shadrach, Meshach and Abednego in the fiery furnace, Daniel in the lion's den, Abraham when he was called to go out to the place which he would receive as an inheritance. The building of the ark that saved Noah was an accomplishment made possible "by faith."

When an individual truly has faith in God he will obey without hesitation, regardless of how demanding the task might seem. Noah was commanded to build an ark.

I'm speculating when I say if God was to command one of us to build an Ark the response would go something like this: "You want me to build what? An Ark? You have got to be crazy!! Where am I going to get the money? Do you have any idea how much something that big would cost? And anyway, it doesn't look like rain!"

I couldn't help but wonder, why did the Holy Spirit, in the New Testament Scriptures, call our attention way back to Noah and the other faithful men and women of long ago?

Could it be because the characteristics of the faith that saved Noah, are the same as what our faith needs to have today? It was not "faith alone" but an obedient faith. None of the many examples of faith listed in Hebrews 11 were examples of faith alone. None of them! But let us focus on Noah, and his faith.

If Noah was **480 years old** when God told him to build an Ark and 600 when the flood came, it is reasonable to assume that the construction of the Ark took place during this **120-year** period (See Gen. 6:3 along with I Pet. 3:20).

171

We will indeed see the parallels we are meant to see and be granted a better understanding of what our faith needs to be. Think about it. God tells Noah to build an Ark. I didn't see anywhere in the bible that Noah complained. I didn't see anywhere in the bible where Noah asked who was going to pay for the Ark, or where the materials would come from. Rain was not in the forecast; it didn't look like rain and not a cloud in the sky. Yet, Noah set out to build the Ark by faith.

Faith and the Future

To Noah, what God said was going to happen was real, though yet unseen. Things are not necessarily "unreal" just because they are "unseen." In fact, the most important parts of reality are unseen. Love and hate are both powerful motivators, and while the effects of both can be seen, no one can see love or hate itself. In fact, everything we see is only temporary. 2 Corinthians 4:18: "While we do not look at the things which are seen, but at the things which are not seen. For the things which are seen are temporary, but the things which are not seen are eternal."

"Blind faith" is accepting that something is true, without having seen it or, evidence of it at all. On the other hand, "faith" is our acceptance and response to something we have not seen, but we have seen evidence that causes us to accept it as true. Our faith in God is based on evidence, but it is still faith because we have not seen God Himself (Hebrews 11:1).

Noah had the faith to believe in a future that had never happened before! Why did he believe something was going to happen that had never happened before? Did he have evidence that it would? Yes! His "evidence" was that he served the true and living God and the creator of all things.

When God told Noah of His decision, Noah believed it based upon who he knew God to be. It is a dangerous thing to think that something will not happen because it has never happened before.

That mentality worked against the people of Noah's day who dismissed the idea of the flood to come. Can I share with you that today, people are making the same mistake in not preparing themselves for the Lord's return, and the final day of this physical realm (2 Peter 3:1-9)? It's better to accept that if God says something will happen, it will, even if it has never happened before.

Faith Actively Responds to the Future

It is a mistake to believe in God but to postpone responding to His promises and warnings. This is especially true considering that the most important things are unseen and eternal, and we put everything in serious jeopardy by such neglect. When disaster strikes, the severity of the effect is increased because we tend to respond too late. America could have been ready for Pearl Harbor, hurricane Katrina, or the World Trade Center terrorist actions. This kind of late reaction seems far too typical of us, The United States of America.

But saving faith calls for decisive action in the present (James 2:14-26). If we delay our response to the Lord and His promises and warnings until His coming is upon us, then it will become simply impossible to "catch up." We will be lost. Faith is not something we merely think about, it's a thing we do something about! Noah built an ark, obeying God in everything (Genesis 6:22).

God has given other commands and instructions to us as well. Our response to these should be like Noah's was. We shall prepare by obeying God in everything.

Faith Grows Endurance

Righteous men and women often are on the receiving end of taunts and reproaches. But listen! Reproach for having obeyed God should be the least of our worries. In fact, it should be a source of rejoicing (Matthew 10:24-33; 5:10-12)!

Like Noah, and like the Lord Himself, we need to patiently endure such criticism. Noah urged the people of his day to repent as he preached God's righteousness, but they refused (2 Peter 2:5).

Up until the time of the flood, they continued to live as if they had nothing to be concerned about (Matthew 24:37-39). Were those who scoffed prepared for the flood? Noah was! Will those who mock today, be prepared for the Lord's return and judgment? We will be!

Faith and Obedience

Noah did not modify what God told him to do (Genesis 6:22; 15). It is very important for us to do all things "according to the pattern" as well (Hebrews 8:5). Would Noah and his family have been saved from the flood if he had built the ark 310 cubits long? God commanded 300 cubits, but that is such a slight difference. Would it matter? Did God have to tell Noah, "Do not build the ark 310 cubits long?" Noah was not concerned about such questions. He simply obeyed. God's specifics, as well as His silence, is significant and must be respected (Hebrews 7:11-14).

Faith Saves!

The quality of faith exhibited by Noah is the only kind that saves. These examples from before Christ were written down in the Old Testament, and then the Hebrew writer refers to them in the New Testament, to show us what saving faith is all about.

Concerning Noah's obedience of faith, and the destruction of the ancient world by flood, notice what Peter wrote: "who once were disobedient, when the patience of God kept waiting in the days of Noah, during the construction of the ark, in which a few, that is, eight persons, were brought safely through the water. Corresponding to that, baptism now saves you (not the removal of dirt from the flesh, but an appeal to God for a good conscience) through the resurrection of Jesus Christ, who is at the right hand of God, having gone into heaven, after angels and authorities and powers had been subjected to Him" (1 Peter 3:20-22).

We need faith like Noah had, and as much as Noah needed it. Noah's faith was an obedient trust in God. Does our own faith have the characteristics of the faith that saved Noah?

Noah's faith obeyed God's commands, thus preparing him for the coming judgment. We are warned by Peter: "The world at that time was destroyed, being flooded with water. But the present heavens and earth by His word are being reserved for fire, kept for the Day of Judgment and destruction of ungodly men" (2 Peter 3:6-7). Is your faith moving you to prepare for the future?

By faith, Noah, warned by God about events yet unseen, built an ark to save his household, thereby condemning the world and becoming an heir to the righteousness that is in accordance with faith.

Notes: _____

_____

_____

_____

_____

_____

_____

_____

_____

_____

_____

_____

_____

_____

_____

_____

It's Time to Rejoice

1 Thessalonians 5:16-18 (NKJV)

[16]Rejoice always, [17] pray without ceasing, [18] in everything give thanks, for this is the will of God in Christ Jesus for you."

Paul reminds us to rejoice, always. The Bible calls us to rejoice always and give thanks in all circumstances, in afflictions as well as times of blessing. To rejoice in all things doesn't mean that we rejoice that someone dies or is diagnosed with cancer. To rejoice in all things means that we believe God is doing glorious things in and through all our circumstances, and even turns evil to good for those who love Christ.

To rejoice and give thanks in everything isn't simply a good idea – it is critical and important. Why?? Because: God commands us to rejoice. God doesn't command us to do anything without a reason. All his commands are intended to bring blessings into our lives.

Rejoicing is important for it is a way to lift our eyes to heaven and set our minds on things above.

Rejoicing in all things helps us avoid thinking hard thoughts of God.

Rejoicing in affliction reminds us that God causes all things to work together for our greatest good – to make us like Christ.

Rejoicing in all things speaks powerfully to both believers and unbelievers. Remember Paul and Silas singing hymns while in stocks in prison and the other prisoners were listening and suddenly there was such a violent earthquake that the foundations of the prison were shaken (Acts 16.24-25).

Rejoicing helps prevent us from grumbling and complaining.

Rejoicing in affliction strengthens our faith in God's character and promises.

Rejoicing opens the door for us to experience deep, genuine joy in Christ.

176

Rejoicing in all things helps us ward off self-pity.

Rejoicing in all things says that Christ is our source of joy and delight, not our circumstances.

Rejoicing in all things says that we believe God is wise, good, and loving in his plans for our lives.

Rejoicing in all things glorifies God– it is easy to praise God when all is going well; but it especially honors him when we praise him in the midst of trials.

Rejoice in Jesus today. Give him thanks no matter what you encounter. Not one thing will happen to you that he hasn't ordained for your good.

Paul's command in 1 Thessalonians 5:17 to "pray without ceasing," can be confusing. Obviously, it cannot mean we are to be in a head-bowed, eyes-closed posture all day long. Paul is not referring to non-stop talking, but rather an attitude of God-consciousness and God-surrender that we carry with us all the time. Every waking moment is to be lived in an awareness that God is with us and that He is actively involved and engaged in our thoughts and actions.

When our thoughts turn to worry, fear, discouragement, and anger, we are to consciously and quickly turn every thought into prayer and every prayer into thanksgiving. In his letter to the Philippians, Paul commands us to stop being anxious and instead, "in everything, by prayer and petition, with thanksgiving, present your requests to God" (Philippians 4:6). He taught the believers at Colossae to devote themselves "to prayer, being watchful and thankful" (Colossians 4:2). Paul exhorted the Ephesian believers to see prayer as a weapon to use in fighting spiritual battles (Ephesians 6:18). As we go through the day, prayer should be our first response to every fearful situation, every anxious thought, and every undesired task that God commands. A lack of prayer will cause us to depend on ourselves instead of depending on God's grace. Unceasing prayer is, in essence, continual dependence upon and communion with the Father.

For Christians, prayer should be like breathing. You do not have to think to breathe because the atmosphere exerts pressure on your lungs and essentially forces you to breathe. That is why it is more difficult to hold your breath than it is to breathe. Similarly, when we are born into the family of God, we enter into a spiritual atmosphere where God's presence and grace exert pressure, or influence, on our lives. Prayer is the normal response to that pressure. As believers, we have all entered the divine atmosphere to breathe the air of prayer.

Unfortunately, many believers hold their "spiritual breath" for long periods, thinking brief moments with God are sufficient to allow them to survive. But such restricting of their spiritual intake is caused by sinful desires. The fact is that every believer must be continually in the presence of God, constantly breathing in His truths, to be fully functional.

It is easier for Christians to feel secure by presuming, instead of depending on God's grace. Too many believers become satisfied with physical blessings and have little desire for spiritual ones. When programs, methods, and money produce impressive results, there is an inclination to confuse human success with divine blessings. When that happens, passionate longing for God and yearning for His help will be missing. Continual, persistent, incessant prayer is an essential part of Christian living and flows out of humility and dependence on God.

In the U.S., we celebrate a day of thanksgiving once a year. But God wants us to be intentional about our thankfulness every day. He wants us to develop this spiritual habit, one that is reflected in the life of a radical believer. The truth is, the more deeply you understand God's love, the more grateful you're going to be. What does it mean to be radically grateful? The Bible says, in 1 Thessalonians 5:18: "Give thanks in all circumstances; for this is God's will for you in Christ Jesus" (NIV). In all circumstances give thanks because it's God's will for you.

1 Peter 4:12-13: "Beloved, do not think it strange concerning the fiery trial which is to try you, as though some strange thing happened to you; [13] but rejoice to the extent that you partake of Christ's sufferings,

that when His glory is revealed, you may also be glad with exceeding joy."

You can thank God in every circumstance because God is in control. He can bring good out of evil. He can turn around the mistakes we made. No matter what happens, God isn't going to stop loving us.

That's one reason we should never stop praying. Never stop praying means not giving up. Being thankful means you recognize God is sovereign and can redeem any situation. If we are going to pray without ceasing, we must have Faith in God for what we are praying for in order for God to grant our request.

In 1Thessalonians 5:16-18 we are told to: "Rejoice evermore. Pray without ceasing. In everything give thanks: for this is the will of God in Christ Jesus concerning you." The Lord tells us here that we are to have an attitude of joy, thanksgiving and prayer at all times, no matter what the conditions or circumstances are that surround us.

This verse does not mean that we are to thank God for bad things and tragedies that come our way. It means that we are to remain joyful no matter what is happening in our lives because we have the Lord, and in Him we shall overcome, no matter what the devil is trying to do to us.

The Lord does not want us to thank Him for the bad things that happen to us because He did not send them. He is not the author of evil. We are not to become bitter over life's circumstances, but rather to continue to rejoice in the Lord. It is the will of God for us to rejoice no matter what comes.

It is not the will of God to receive evil things as if from Him. It is an insult to God to thank Him for accidents, sickness, tragedy, etc. God does not send those things to us, the devil does. We are told to resist the devil and submit to God. James 4:7 reads, "Submit yourselves therefore to God. Resist the devil, and he will flee from you." We are to love and rejoice in the Lord despite what the devil tries to do to us.

In closing, I realize it's hard to rejoice when the hell hounds are on your back and you're faced with storm after storm. Storms will come whether in the form of an illness, persecution, financial distress, family problems or in other situations. That's life. Sooner or later your faith will be tested, and you will need peace that transcends understanding. This peace is available to all believers. Through the Holy Spirit, there's an assurance of the peace of God in any storm. Thank God today that you can have peace in the midst of great stress and trials. No matter what we go through, our prayers should be in an attitude of praise even in the midst of our trials. So I say, "Rejoice in the Lord always, Again I say Rejoice!"

Notes: _____

_____

_____

_____

_____

_____

_____

_____

_____

_____

_____

_____

_____

Jesus Can Change Your Situation

John 5:5-9 (NKJV)

⁵Now a certain man was there who had an infirmity thirty-eight years. ⁶When Jesus saw him lying there, and knew that he already had been in that condition a long time, He said to him, 'Do you want to be made well?' ⁷The sick man answered Him, 'Sir, I have no man to put me into the pool when the water is stirred up; but while I am coming, another steps down before me.' ⁸Jesus said to him, 'Rise, take up your bed and walk.' ⁹And immediately the man was made well, took up his bed, and walked.

In Jerusalem, there was a gate in the city called the Sheep Gate. That was where the sheep that were to be sacrificed in the temple were brought into the city. The building of this gate is mentioned in Nehemiah 3:1, 32; 12:39, and thought to be located near the northeast corner of the city.

John says that by the Sheep Gate there was a pool of water called, in Hebrew, "Bethesda." Bethesda means a house of kindness, grace, or mercy.

Gathered around the pool were many people with various ailments such as the blind, crippled or lame, and those who had palsy that withered up some part of their body. This pool was supplied by water from underground springs. We are not told what it was used for other than the tradition that at times, an angel would "trouble" or stir up the waters.

The belief was that an angel would come and stir up the waters and the first person who entered the pool, when waters were stirred up would be healed of their infirmities. Nothing like this is recorded in the Bible and it is believed to have been more of a tradition than fact. The source of the myth could have come from the waters of the pool having a mineral content with medicinal properties.

The waters of the spring would be occasionally agitated by the release of these minerals and healing effect. John states the belief of those gathered at the pool without an explanation, so we just do not know. What is important is that those who were present believed they could be healed if they were the first into the pool. The lame man, like others, was there hoping to be healed.

Those who have chronic diseases will go to great lengths to find relief and healing. When Jesus approached the pool, he saw a man there who had been crippled for thirty-eight years. Jesus, being omniscient, knew the man had been there a long time and asked him if he wanted to be whole.

That question is an important one for those who have physical infirmities, but more importantly for those who, being lost in their sins, have the need of being made spiritually whole. Jesus Christ came into the world to save sinners and whosoever will believe in Him will be saved. But throughout the ages few have been saved. The reason is because most do not want to be spiritually cleansed.

Healing only comes for those who want it. This man wanted to be healed and he was patiently waiting by the pool. Evidently, the man could get around to some degree, but was not fast enough to be the first into the pool. This had happened several times before, but it showed the man had character in his persistence. He kept trying and did not give up. This lets us know that no matter how bad you may think things are, don't give up!

As difficult as the task was in getting up and getting into the pool, this man was not deterred. The man could have said, "It is no use. I will go home and die." God had a plan for this man.

Some might suppose that God imposed His will on the lame man and made him persistent, but a better explanation is that God knew the man's character, and this made his healing possible. This does not mean the man deserved to be healed, but the man exercised a great faith in the healing properties of the pool. Jesus knew the man's humility and saw this was fertile ground for receiving saving faith. Of all those by the pool desiring to be healed, Jesus only chose this man.

Instantly, as Jesus spoke the words, the man was completely healed. To show he was fully healed, Jesus told him to pick up his bed and walk. He did not need to go to "rehab" to learn to walk again. He was healed, mind and body, and such is a true miracle healing by God.

There are many in the church today who wait, metaphorically speaking, by the pool of Bethesda, hoping to be carried into the healing waters. Other Saints might suffer from the isolation of depression or addiction. Widows and widowers live alone or face failing health; families feel devastated by a child's illness or an unexpected accident; and caregivers work long, lonely hours taking care of a family member. Who will carry these infirmed to the pool?

Jesus provided distinctive examples during His visit to the pool that can serve as guidelines to us in ministering to the sick and afflicted:

Jesus looked for one in need. Isn't it interesting that Jesus Christ made it a point to visit the pool of Bethesda during Passover? At a time when He could have focused solely on the rituals and activities of the Jewish holy days, He looked to help those who were in need.

Jesus listens without criticism. In John 5:6, we learn that Jesus saw the infirmed man "and knew that he had been crippled for a long time." Jesus allowed the man to explain his situation and his need. Because we are not omniscient, we need to first listen—and do so without being critical.

Often, what is needed most is for us to be prayerful and to listen without giving advice. People who are suffering don't need our explanations. Sometimes people just need someone to listen to their story or situation without being critical. Growing up I was told, "if you don't know what to say, don't say anything." Even if such comments are said with the best of intentions, sometimes they are best left unsaid.

When we are prayerful, the Spirit can help us know what to say. In doing so, we are listening and responding in a Christlike way.

Jesus serves anonymously. After Jesus healed the man at the pool of Bethesda, the man took up his bed and walked. Jesus did nothing to bring glory to Himself, but in all things glorified the Father, setting the perfect example. Many inside and outside the Church give of their time, talents, and other resources anonymously, not looking for anything in return.

Jesus followed up with the sufferer. After Jesus healed the man at the pool of Bethesda, He sought him out at the temple (John 5:14). Jesus then forgave the man of his sins. At that point, the healed man finally knew who cured him. Jesus Christ, who had already done so much for this man, made it a point to seek him out again and cure him of an even more serious illness: his sins. As a result, complete healing occurred.

Finally, no tragedy happens in a vacuum. Every person experiencing a life-threatening disease, natural disaster, or grief, has family members and friends who are directly affected. They too need help and healing.

Jesus performed many miracles during His earthly ministry, including the one He performed at Bethesda. Ultimately, healing comes from the Savior Himself, but we can help continue His work of making people whole, as we minister to those who face sickness, grief, or disabilities. By using the Savior as our guiding light, we too can learn to find a need, listen without criticism, give anonymously, learn about disease and grief, and follow up with the sufferer.

Prayer is no doubt one of the best things we can do. We should pray, read Scriptures, and listen to prayer requests, praise reports, and testimonies. This reminds us not to give up on the things we're praying for. Delay is not denial. This man, at the pool of Bethesda, had been crippled for thirty-eight long years, but he did not give up and Jesus healed him. Jesus can change your situation and faith in God will heal the sick.

Notes: _____

_____

_____

_____

_____

_____

_____

_____

_____

_____

_____

_____

_____

_____

_____

_____

_____

_____

_____

_____

Working for the Lord Will Pay Off After While

Luke 10:1-9 (NLT)

[1]The Lord now chose seventy-two other disciples and sent them ahead in pairs to all the towns and places he planned to visit. [2]These were his instructions to them: "The harvest is great, but the workers are few. So pray to the Lord who is in charge of the harvest; ask him to send more workers into his fields. [3]Now go, and remember that I am sending you out as lambs among wolves. [4]Don't take any money with you, nor a traveler's bag, nor an extra pair of sandals. And don't stop to greet anyone on the road. [5]Whenever you enter someone's home, first say, 'May God's peace be on this house.' [6]If those who live there are peaceful, the blessing will stand; if they are not, the blessing will return to you. [7]Don't move around from home to home. Stay in one place, eating and drinking what they provide. Don't hesitate to accept hospitality, because those who work deserve their pay. [8]If you enter a town and it welcomes you, eat whatever is set before you. [9]Heal the sick, and tell them, 'The Kingdom of God is near you now.'

In Chapter 10:1, Jesus has now chosen seventy-two other disciples and sent them ahead to all the towns and places He planned to visit. Some versions say seventy. The numbers 72 or 70 represented the nations of the world. The point is, the good news is for both Jews and Gentiles.

He sent them out two by two. This suggests competent testimony. In 2 Corinthians 13:1b it says, "In the mouth of two or three witnesses every word shall be established."

The mission of the twelve disciples represented Jesus' ministry to Israel. This mission represented his outreach to the Gentiles.

These were his instructions to them: "The harvest is great, but the workers are few; so pray to the Lord who is in charge of the harvest; ask him to send more workers into his fields." In the past when I've read this Scripture, I assumed the harvest was the people already in church not doing anything. But in my reading and research, the harvest here refers to people who need to hear the Good News and be gathered to God's presence. There are so many unchurched people in the world, and we need to do a better job reaching them and sharing the Good News. The Lord's servants should pray constantly. Pray that He will send out laborers into His harvest field. The need is always greater than the supply of workers. In praying for laborers, we must be willing to go ourselves.

[3] "Now go, and remember that I am sending you out as lambs among wolves." The disciples of Jesus are sent forth into a hostile environment. They are, to outward appearances, like defenseless lambs among wolves. They cannot expect to be treated royally by the world, but rather to be persecuted and even killed. Jesus' followers are not to dominate others, but to sacrifice themselves for the benefit of others, remembering that God, the Good Shepherd, protects them from the wolves.

[4] "Don't take any money with you, nor a traveler's bag, nor an extra pair of sandals. And don't stop to greet anyone on the road." Considerations of personal comfort are not to be permitted. Carry neither moneybag or traveler's bag nor sandals. The moneybag speaks of financial reserves, the traveler's bag suggests food reserves. The sandals may refer either to an extra pair or footgear affording comfort. All three speak of the poverty which, though having nothing yet, possesses all things and makes many rich. In other words, the disciples were to depend on God and on the help of those whom they served. This is not being antisocial, but is staying focused on the task Jesus had given them.

In verse 4b Jesus told them not to stop to greet anyone on the road. Christ's servants are not to waste time on long ceremonious greetings, such as were common in the East. They were to be curious and civil; they must use their time in the glorious proclamation of the gospel rather than in profitless talk. There was no time for needless delays.

In a time where violence, fighting, stress and loneliness enter our homes in so many ways, we must pray for peace, protection, and wellbeing on the places we live. When Jesus sent his friends into towns and villages to stay in people's homes and do his good work, he told them to always bless the homes they enter. [5] "Whenever you enter someone's home, first say, 'May God's peace be on this house.' God's peace means spiritual blessings and wholeness.

[6] "If those who live there are peaceful, the blessing will stand; if they are not, the blessing will return to you." In other words, if the initial greetings are favorably received, then the host is a son of peace. If the disciples are refused, they should not be discouraged; their peace will return to them again. There has been no waste or loss and others will receive it.

[7] "Don't move around from home to home. Stay in one place, eating and drinking what they provide. Don't hesitate to accept hospitality, because those who work deserve their pay." Jesus wanted them to stay in the same house because the people might characterize them as those who are shopping for the most luxurious accommodations, whereas they should live simply and gratefully.

[8] "If you enter a town and it welcomes you, eat whatever is set before you." The disciples should not hesitate to eat whatever food and drinks are offered to them. As servants of the Lord, they are entitled to their upkeep.

[9] "Heal the sick, and tell them, 'The Kingdom of God is near you now.'" Back then cities and towns took a position either for or against the Lord, just as individuals do. If an area is receptive to the message, the disciples should preach there, accept its hospitality, and bring the blessings of the gospel to it. Christ's servants should eat such things as are set before them, not being hard to please about their food, or causing inconvenience in the home. After all, food is not the main thing in their lives. Jesus gave the same mission to the twelve disciples, to announce the Kingdom of God, and to demonstrate its authority by casting out demons and healing the sick. Jesus was training the disciples to carry on His work after he was gone.

Just as Jesus sent disciples out over two thousand years ago, He is still sending disciples out today. In order for us to be effective disciples today, we must grow in our relationship with Jesus.

Growing in our relationship with Jesus means to know Him better, to love and obey Him more. Matthew 22:37-38 reads, "Jesus replied: 'You must love the Lord your God with all your heart, all your soul, and all your mind.' This is the first and greatest commandment."

Your growing love for God will lead you to obey His commandments.

John 14:21 reads, "Those who obey my commandments are the ones who love me. And because they love me, my Father will love them, and I will love them. And I will reveal myself to each one of them."

Just as it's natural for a child to grow in a loving relationship with a parent, it is also natural for you to grow in your love relationship with God. Communication is vital to any relationship.

Here are four aspects of communication that will help us develop our relationship with Jesus.

1. **God communicates with us through the Bible, revealing His character and His will.**

   2 Timothy 3:16-17: "All Scripture is inspired by God and is useful to teach us what is true and to make us realize what is wrong in our lives. It straightens us out and teaches us to do what is right. It is God's way of preparing us in every way, fully equipped for every good thing God wants us to do."

2. **We communicate with God through prayer, sharing our thoughts, our needs, and our desire to do His will. These verses tell us we can pray about everything. When we pray according to God's will, He hears us and answers us. Thanking God is also part of praying.**

   Philippians 4:6-7: "Don't worry about anything; instead, pray about everything. Tell God what you need and thank him for all he has done. If you do this, you will experience God's peace, which is far more wonderful than the human mind can understand. His peace will guard your hearts and minds as you live in Christ Jesus."

1 John 5:14-15: "And we can be confident that he will listen to us whenever we ask him for anything in line with his will. And if we know he is listening when we make our requests, we can be sure that he will give us what we ask for."

1 Thessalonians 5:18: "No matter what happens, always be thankful, for this is God's will for you who belong to Christ Jesus."

Ephesians 5:20 reads, "And you will always give thanks for everything to God the Father in the name of our Lord Jesus Christ."

3. **We communicate with Christians through fellowship, encouraging and building up one another.**

It is important to spend time with other Christians to encourage each other to love and do good. We need to share our Christian experience with others who love God, and likewise allow them to share with us. God appoints the church as a place for us to meet other Christians and learn about God. Bible Study, Prayer Service, Church School, and other meetings are also helpful.

(Hebrews 10:24-25): "Think of ways to encourage one another to outbursts of love and good deeds. And let us not neglect our meeting together, as some people do, but encourage and warn each other, especially now that the day of his coming back again is drawing near."

4. **We communicate with others who don't know God personally by sharing our relationship with Jesus.**

Acts 4:12 reads, "There is salvation in no one else! There is no other name in all of heaven for people to call on to save them."

God is still moving and if we want to catch the movement of God, we must pack light and move fast. May God continue to bless you and keep you is my prayer. Amen.

Notes: _____

_____

_____

_____

_____

_____

_____

_____

_____

_____

_____

_____

_____

_____

_____

_____

_____

_____

_____

_____

_____

_____

Palm Sunday

Hebrews 9:19-22 (ESV)

[19]For when every commandment of the law had been declared by Moses to all the people, he took the blood of calves and goats, with water and scarlet wool and hyssop, and sprinkled both the book itself and all the people, [20] saying, 'This is the blood of the covenant that God commanded for you.' [21]And in the same way he sprinkled with the blood both the tent and all the vessels used in worship. [22] Indeed, under the law almost everything is purified with blood, and without the shedding of blood there is no forgiveness of sins.

The Bible reveals that when Jesus entered Jerusalem, the crowds greeted him by waving palm branches and covering his path with palm branches. Then the multitudes who went before, and those who followed cried out, saying: "Hosanna to the Son of David! 'Blessed is He who comes in the name of the LORD!' Hosanna in the highest!"

Immediately, following this great time of celebration in the ministry of Jesus, he begins his journey to the cross.

The biblical account of Palm Sunday can be found in Matthew 21:1-11; Mark 11:1-11; Luke 19:28-44; and John 12:12-19.

Have you ever wondered why Jesus had to die? I mean, this is God's Son! Surely God could have come up with something better than death. If not, couldn't God have come up with an easier death? Dying on a cross is just a horrific death. Maybe Jesus could have died in his old age or in his sleep. I want to focus on the last part of verse 22: "And without the shedding of blood there is no forgiveness of sins."

"When Moses had proclaimed every commandment of the law to all the people, he took the blood of calves, together with water, scarlet wool and branches of hyssop, and sprinkled the scroll and all the people."

Both the Old and New Covenants were put into effect by blood. The blood proved the death, thereby enforcing and enacting the will of the one who died (Hebrews 9:17). Leviticus 17:11 explains why the blood was used: "For the life of a creature is in the blood, and I have given it to you to make atonement for yourselves on the altar; it is the blood that makes atonement for one's life." **So it was necessary for both Covenants to be ushered in by blood.** First, it proved the death, because the blood is the life force. And second, without it, there could be no forgiveness for sins.

Jesus' blood was shed to usher in the New Covenant. His blood proved that a death had occurred thereby enacting His last will and testament. His blood was the price necessary for this will to come to pass. In other words, it put this covenant into effect. **The New Covenant is not only the will of Jesus whose blood ushered it in; it is also the will of God.**

Throughout Jesus' time on earth, He said over and over that His will was to do the will of the Father (John 6:38). He stressed that what He said was only what the Father told Him to say (John 8:28), and He did only what He saw the Father do (John 5:19). His words and teachings were not His own, but from the One who sent Him (John 7:16).

In fact, John 6:38 summarizes this very nicely: "For I have come down from heaven not to do my will but to do the will of him who sent me." The writer of Hebrews starts chapter one by declaring that Jesus is the exact representation of God the Father (Hebrews 1:3). Since they are one and the same, we can see that Jesus' blood was the life force that was able to usher in the will of God, which was the New Covenant.

Not only did Jesus' blood prove the death and put the Covenant into effect, but part of the New Covenant that God spoke of through the prophets included the forgiveness of sins (Jeremiah 31: 31-34; Isaiah 54:13; Hebrews 8: 8-12; Hebrews 10: 16-18; Leviticus 17: 11). The life force is in the blood, and this is used as a means for atonement. **Jesus' blood served multiple purposes. It enacted the Will of the Covenant, and it was the cleansing agent for sin**. If no blood was shed, there couldn't be any forgiveness for sins.

The "blood" of Christ, which betokens His death by the shedding of His "blood" in expiatory sacrifice; to drink His "blood" is to appropriate the saving effects of His expiatory death" (John 6:53). As "the life of the flesh is in the blood" (Leviticus 17:11) and was forfeited by sin, **life eternal can be imparted only by the act of making atonement, in the giving up of the life by the sinless Savior.**

In other words, life had been forfeited because of sin, which is why Jesus' life was given so that He, as a sinless man, could impart eternal life through this sacrifice. Jesus himself said, *53*"I tell you the truth, **unless you eat the flesh of the Son of Man and drink his blood, you have no life in you.**"

54"Whoever eats my flesh and **drinks my blood has eternal life,** and I will raise him up at the last day" (John 6:53-54). **Our life was forfeited because of sin, but Jesus' blood was shed to forgive and restore us to a state, as if we had never sinned in the first place.** What an amazing truth!

Jesus didn't just give His blood; He let it flow freely. In fact, it didn't stop until every last drop had been given. He was poured out unto death, which is what Isaiah prophesied about Him, "Therefore I will give him a portion among the great, and he will divide the spoils with the strong, **because he poured out his life unto death,** and was numbered with the transgressors. **For he bore the sin of many, and made intercession for the transgressors**" (Isaiah 5:3:12). His life force completely covered, cleansed, and annulled sin. Our lives had been forfeited because of sin; however, His blood completely reversed the effect of sin so that we could experience eternal life.

Jesus understood this, which is why He spoke these words while reclining at the table with His disciples at the last supper. "Then he took the cup, gave thanks and offered it to them, saying, **"Drink from it, all of you. This is my blood of the covenant, which is poured out for many for the forgiveness of sins"** (Matthew 26:27-28). **He knew the price to bring us to the Father and His own words testify to the fact that He would let the blood flow freely.** He knew His blood would usher in the covenant and it would completely and utterly blot out and destroy the effects and stains of sins.

His perfect blood was shed to usher in both the New Covenant and the forgiveness of sins. Neither one could be accomplished without it, which is why He freely gave himself to the will of God. Jesus accomplished what we could not, and because of His sacrifice we have been forgiven, freed and offered eternal life through the person of Jesus Christ.

As we look forward to Easter Sunday, take some time this week and reflect on all Jesus went through for us. And remember, God sent his Son. They called him Jesus. He came to love, heal, and forgive. He lived and died, to buy our pardon. An empty grave is there to prove our savior lives.

And because He lives, we can face tomorrow,

because He lives all fear is gone,

because we know who holds the future, life is worth living,

because He lives.

Notes: _____

_____

_____

_____

_____

_____

_____

_____

_____

New Life in Christ

2 Corinthians 5:14-19 (NKJV)

[14]For the love of Christ compels us, because we judge thus: that if one died for all, then all died; [15]and He died for all, that those who live should live no longer for themselves, but for Him who died for them and rose again. [16]Therefore, from now on, we regard no one according to the flesh. Even though we have known Christ according to the flesh, yet now we know *Him* thus no longer. [17]Therefore, if anyone *is* in Christ, *he is* a new creation; old things have passed away; behold, all things have become new. [18]Now all things are of God, who has reconciled us to Himself through Jesus Christ, and has given us the ministry of reconciliation, [19]that is, that God was in Christ reconciling the world to Himself, not imputing their trespasses to them, and has committed to us the word of reconciliation.

Choirs sometimes sing a song entitled "Brand New Life." The lyrics are:

I moved from my old house
I moved from my old friends
I moved from my old way of strife
Thank God I moved out to a brand new life

He changed my old way with words
He changed my old leveled mind
He changed my heart and gave me a new start
Thank God I moved out to a brand new life

Can't you see I'm a new man
Don't you know I got a new name
And one day I'll live in that new land
Because I moved out to a brand new life

The new creation is described in 2 Corinthians 5:17: "Therefore, if anyone is in Christ, he is a new creation; the old has gone, the new has come!"

The words "therefore" refer us back to verses 14-16 where Paul tells us that all believers have died with Christ and no longer live for themselves. Galatians 2:20 (NKJV) reads: "I have been crucified with Christ; it is no longer I who live, but Christ lives in me; and the *life* which I now live in the flesh I live by faith in the Son of God, who loved me and gave Himself for me."

Our lives are no longer worldly; they are now spiritual. Our "death" is that of the old sin nature which was nailed to the cross with Christ. (Romans 6:4): "Therefore we were buried with Him through baptism into death, that just as Christ was raised from the dead by the glory of the Father, even so we also should walk in newness of life."

That new person that was raised up is what Paul refers to in 2 Corinthians 5:17 as the "new creation."

To understand the new creation, first we must grasp that it is in fact a creation, something created by God. John 1:13 tells us that this new birth was brought about by the will of God. We did not inherit the new nature, nor did we decide to re-create ourselves anew, nor did God simply clean up our old nature; God created something entirely fresh and unique.

First, the new creation is completely new, brought about from nothing, just as the whole universe was created by God from nothing. Only the Creator could accomplish such an act.

Second, "old things have passed away." The "old" refers to everything that is part of our old nature—natural pride, love of sin, reliance on works, and our former opinions, habits, and passions.

Most significantly, what we loved has passed away, especially the supreme love of self and with it, self-righteousness, self-promotion, and self-justification. The new creature looks outwardly toward Christ instead of inwardly toward self. The old things died, nailed to the cross with our sin nature.

Along with the old passing away, "the new has come!" Old, dead things are replaced with new things, full of life and the glory of God.

The newborn soul delights in the things of God and dislikes the things of the world and the flesh.

Our purposes, feelings, desires, and understandings are fresh and different. We see the world differently. The Bible seems to be a new book, and though we may have read it before, there is a beauty about it which we never saw before, and which we wonder at not having perceived.

The whole face of nature seems to us to be changed, and we seem to be in a new world. The heavens and the earth are filled with new wonders, and all things seem now to speak forth the praise of God. There are new feelings toward all people—a new kind of love toward family and friends, a new compassion never before felt for enemies, and a new love for all mankind. The things we once loved, we now detest. The sin we once held onto, we now desire to put away forever. We "put off the old man with his deeds" (Colossians 3:9). And put on the "new self-created to be like God in true righteousness and holiness" (Ephesians 4:24).

What about the Christian who continues to sin? There is a difference between continuing to sin and continuing to live in sin. No one reaches sinless perfection in this life, but the redeemed Christian is being sanctified (made holy) day by day, sinning less and hating it more each time he fails. You've heard the song:

I am redeemed, bought with a price,
Jesus has changed my whole life.
If anybody asks you, just who I am,
tell them I am redeemed.

He purchased my salvation
with His own precious blood
He purchased my life for me
I'm walking, oh I'm walking with Jesus, I'm a child of the King
And it's all because I'm redeemed.

Yes, we still sin, but unwillingly and less frequently as we mature. Our new self hates the sin that still has a hold on us. The difference is that the new creation is no longer a slave to sin, as we formerly were.

We are now freed from sin and it no longer has power over us. Now we are empowered by, and for righteousness. We now have the choice to "let sin reign" or to count ourselves "dead to sin but alive to God in Christ Jesus." Best of all, now we have the power to choose the latter.

The new creation life is supposed to be a life lived by faith. Romans 1:17 says, "For in it the righteousness of God is revealed from faith to faith; as it is written, "The just shall live by faith."

Ephesians 2: 8-9: "For by grace you have been saved through faith, and that not of yourselves; *it is* the gift of God, [9]not of works, lest anyone should boast."

Three important words in these verses explain the basis of our acceptance before God:

GRACE: Unmerited favor, an undeserved gift.

The role grace plays in establishing our relationship with God is we didn't deserve this relationship, nor did we earn it by any good works. Rather, it is a gift from God that we accepted when we received Christ through faith.

SAVED: Rescued, spared from disaster.

Romans 6:23 says that the result of sin is death. When we received Christ, we put our trust in Christ and his death for our sin. We have been rescued from death and eternal separation from God.

FAITH: Belief, trust, commitment of mind, attitude, action.

Simply put, faith is believing or trusting God and his Word. Instead of believing in your own ability to earn God's favor, we must now trust that we have been reconciled to God through what Christ has done for us.

It is by faith that we enter into the Christian life, and it is by faith that we live it out. When we begin the Christian life by coming to Christ for forgiveness of sin, we understand that what we seek cannot be obtained by any other means than by faith. We cannot work our way to heaven because nothing we could ever do would be sufficient. The new creation is a wondrous thing, formed in the mind of God and created by His power and for His glory.

We can be confident in our new relationship with Christ because we have been completely forgiven and accepted by God. Only Christ's death on the cross is sufficient to provide this proper relationship with God.

May God continue to bless you and keep you is my prayer. Amen.

Notes: _____

_____

_____

_____

_____

_____

_____

_____

_____

_____

_____

_____

_____

Send Me, I'll Go

Isaiah 6:8 (NIV)

[8]Then I heard the voice of the Lord saying, "Whom shall I send? And who will go for us?" And I said, "Here Am I. Send Me!

God asks this question, not as if he were unresolved whom to send, but that Isaiah might have an opportunity to voluntarily offer his service. And who will go for us? The Lord spoke in the presence of his angels, the heavenly council, to deliver the following message. The Prophet Isaiah was so overcome by the grace of God in cleansing him that he willingly committed himself to a lifetime of ministry. Here I am. Send me.

Isaiah volunteered to go forth preaching God's Word. This is an awesome passage of Scripture.

This Scripture is the foundation of our Class Leader Creed. "Then I heard a voice of the Lord say, whom shall I send, and who will go for us. And I said, here am I, send me." And it goes on to say, "We as Class Leaders, have been touched, cleaned up and answered to the call of service." Our vision, too, like Isaiah's, has been reinforced and endowed by the spirit of the Lord. This is the nature of our Christian Ministry.

We should have the mind of Isaiah, and say to the Lord, send me, I'll go. If the truth be told, God blesses some people so good that they forget all about the gift God has blessed them with. God has blessed each of us with at least one gift. Romans 12:6-8(NLT): "[6]In his grace, God has given us different gifts for doing certain things well. So if God has given you the ability to prophesy, speak out with as much faith as God has given you. [7]If your gift is serving others, serve them well. If you are a teacher, teach well. [8]If your gift is to encourage others, be encouraging. If it is giving, give generously. If God has given you leadership ability, take the responsibility seriously. And if you have a gift for showing kindness to others, do it gladly." Let's use those gifts to the glory of God. It doesn't matter what people say about you, or what you've done in the past. Romans 3:22-23(NLT): "We are made right with God by placing our faith in Jesus Christ. And this is true for everyone who believes, no matter who we are. [23] For everyone has sinned; and we all fall short of God's glorious standard."

In Isaiah 6:5 (NLT), we find Isaiah acknowledging his transgressions before God, living amongst a sinful and rebellious nation (just like America today). Isaiah 6:5: Then I said, "It's all over! I am doomed, for I am a sinful man. I have filthy lips, and I live among a people with filthy lips. Yet I have seen the King, the LORD of Heaven's Armies." The Prophet Isaiah was so overcome by the grace of God in cleansing him as stated in the seventh verse of this chapter: "With it he touched my mouth and said, 'See, this has touched your lips; your guilt is taken away and your sin atoned for'" (NIV).

Then in verse 8, Isaiah volunteers to serve the Lord, to go forth, preaching the Word of God to Israel. Isaiah cried out to God, *"HERE AM I; SEND ME."*

Our choir sometimes sings a song, *"I'll go if I have to go by myself. I'll sing if I have to sing by myself. I'll pray if I have to pray by myself." Then they say, "send me I'll go." I believe God is just waiting for us to say, "Send me, Lord. I'll go if I have to go by myself."*

But, if you go trusting and believing in God, you're not by yourself, because God said He will never leave us nor forsake us.

What a precious Scripture! I believe every believer should have the same heart's attitude as Isaiah... "I'll go Lord. Here I am, please send me." Romans 10:15: "And how can anyone preach unless they are sent? As it is written: "How beautiful are the feet of those who bring good news!" (NIV)

We have been called to serve. Mark 10:45: "For even the Son of Man did not come to be served, but to serve, and to give His life a ransom for many."

I believe one of the saddest testimonies in the Bible, which is so true in the world today, is found in Philippians 2:20-21 spoken by the frustrated Apostle Paul, [20]For I have no one like-minded, who will sincerely care for your state. [21] For all seek their own, not the things which are of Christ Jesus.

The world hasn't changed in 2,000 years; people are still as selfish today as they were back in Paul's time. It's hard enough to find a genuine born-again Christian, let alone finding a believer who loves Jesus Christ and wants to center their life upon the things of Jesus Christ.

The world is going to Hell. What are you doing about it? Do you care? The truth of the matter is we should care as Christians because God cares and He has asked for you to care too, by committing your life to God. 1st Peter 5:7: Casting all your care upon Him, for He cares for you.

I encourage everyone to allow God to use you. We go through trials, test, ups and downs, peaks and valleys, illness, death of loves ones, loss of jobs, financial problems, marital problems, foreclosure on homes, repossession of automobiles, drug addiction, alcoholism, and a whole lot of other things. Even with all of that, God is still GOOD. If you don't believe me, just take time to visit the hospitals and nursing homes and prisons. James 1:2-3: [2]My brethren, count it all joy when you fall into various trials, [3] knowing that the testing of your faith produces patience.

In closing, there are other Scriptures in the bible to show others going where God wanted them to go. Abraham, who led Isaac on that heartbreaking journey to Mount Moriah, was faithfully going where the Lord wanted him to go (see Genesis 22). So was David when he stepped out before the hosts of Israel to answer the challenge of the giant Goliath (see 1 Samuel 17). Esther, inspired to save her people, walked a life-threatening path to challenge the king in his inner court (see Esther 4–5). "I'll go where you want me to go, dear Lord" was the motivation for Lehi to leave Jerusalem (see 1 Nehemiah 2) and for his son Nephi to return for the precious records (see 1 Nehemiah 3). Hundreds of other scriptural examples can be cited.

It may not be on the mountain height
Or over the stormy sea,

It may not be at the battle's front
My Lord will have need of me.
But if, by a still, small voice he calls
To paths that I do not know,
I'll answer, dear Lord, with my hand in thine:
I'll go where you want me to go.

These words from "I'll Go Where You Want Me to Go" express the commitment of the faithful children of God in all ages.

So the next time God wants to use you, remember Isaiah and say, "Lord, send me. I'll go."

May God continue to bless you and keep you is my prayer.

Notes: _____

_____

_____

_____

_____

_____

_____

_____

_____

_____

_____

_____

Set Apart

Psalm 4:1-3 (NKJV)

[1]Hear me when I call, O God of my righteousness! You have relieved me in my distress; Have mercy on me, and hear my prayer. [2]How long, O you sons of men, Will you turn my glory to shame? How long will you love worthlessness and seek falsehood? But know that the LORD has set apart for Himself him who is godly; The LORD will hear when I call to Him."

Throughout the Scripture, God sets apart people for himself and his purposes. Often the Bible uses the language of holiness to show this act of setting apart. In Psalm 4:3, however, the language is slightly different though the idea is the same. Here, God distinguishes those who are godly because they have received God's faithful love.

In other words, Psalm 4:3 does not mean, if we make ourselves godly, then God will set us apart. Rather, God sets us apart in his mercy, making a covenant with us based on his salvation. He makes us godly so that we might live in a godly manner.

If this seems like a bold statement, it is. The lies of the world will create doubt to make you think you are not special in the eyes of God. The world tells you that it is okay to give into your sinful desires because after all, "you are not perfect." While we are not perfect God tells us to be good, righteous, and holy as He is. Psalm 145:17: "The Lord is righteous in all His ways, Gracious in all His works."

To the world, that is not realistic of what life should be like so it is not surprising that people will doubt you, downgrade your gifts, or even walk away from your relationship with them.

You are called on because God has chosen you specifically out of the world in order to glorify His kingdom. Jeremiah 1:5: "Before I formed you in the womb I knew you, before you were born I set you apart; I appointed you as a prophet to the nations."

But the emphasis in Psalm 4:3 is not upon how we live in our godliness. Rather, this verse underscores the fact that the Lord has set us apart "for himself." We belong to him, not primarily to do his work, but because he loves us and seeks relationships with us. We serve the Lord, therefore, in response to his initiation, and in an intimate relationship with him.

God has set you apart for himself. God wants a relationship with us. He seeks intimacy with us, so that we might know his amazing love.

Sometimes we may pray for something for years and one single cry to God in times of distress brings direction or deliverance instantly.

Many have wondered why there are such powerful results from simply crying out to God, yet the promise is clear: Throughout Scripture, believers are instructed to cry out to God in times of trouble. Here are a few examples:

Psalm 50:15: "Call upon me in the day of trouble: I will deliver thee, and thou shalt glorify me."

Jeremiah 33:3: "'Call to Me, and I will answer you, and show you great and mighty things, which you do not know.'"

Psalm 34:17: "The righteous cry out, and the LORD hears, And delivers them out of all their troubles."

Psalm 56:9: "When I cry out to You, Then my enemies will turn back; This I know, because God is for me."

The second part of this Scripture says, "The Lord will hear when I call to Him." To call upon the Lord is to enjoy the rich presence of His divine Person. I know there are some who don't believe God hears their prayers sometimes. The truth of the matter is, God hears all our prayers.

Imagine this: Jesus walking through the city of Jericho with His disciples, with a very large crowd following them. As He was leaving Jericho, a man by the name of Bartimaeus was sitting by the roadside. Being blind, he had to beg for his sustenance. As the crowd passed by him, he realized that Jesus was among them. My guess is, he had heard a lot about Jesus, even that He could heal the blind. I got excited when I read this because in a sense Bartimaeus was just like we are. We have heard so much about how he healed the sick, how he raised the dead, how he made the lame walk, and the blind to see.

Bartimaeus realized this was his chance. So he yelled out, "Jesus, Son of David, have mercy on me!" Since many from the crowd were telling him to be quiet, I'm thinking Jesus must have been talking to the crowd as they walked, and in order to hear him, the crowd wanted Bartimaeus to shut up, but he kept yelling, not just once, but continuously. Then in Mark 10:49 (NASB), "And Jesus stopped and said, 'Call him here.' So they called the blind man, saying to him, 'Take courage, stand up! He is calling for you.'" I want to place the emphasis on, "And Jesus stopped."

I'm speculating when I say Bartimaeus probably wasn't too important to anyone in the crowd, but his continued cry caused the Son of God to stop in His tracks. Jesus heard someone call His name. Jesus immediately ceased His conversation with the crowd, and probably even turned in the direction of the one calling for Him. This scene in my mind of Jesus walking along, and then suddenly coming to a dead stop because He heard someone call out for Him, has got to be one of the greatest assurances that God hears, not just the crowd, but the individual who calls out for Him. He cares for you and me as an individual person. He knows us by name. He knows all about us.

Crying out to God is an admission of one's need for God. The psalmist declared in Psalm 18:6. "In my distress I called upon the Lord, and cried unto my God: he heard my voice out of his temple, and my cry came before him, even into his ears."

Our cry to God acknowledges God's ability to do what no one else can do. During the storm on the Sea of Galilee, the disciples acknowledged Jesus' power to rescue them when they cried out, "Lord, save us!"

Isn't it amazing that even among the crowds, Jesus makes it personal? He heard the lone voice of Bartimaeus call His name, and stopped what He was doing, and listened to what he had to say.

You may think you're not important, and to a snobby society, you may not be. But to God, you are important – important enough to listen every time you call His name.

Some may say, "I've called out to Him, and nothing has changed." Maybe now, you just need to listen. Is He going to produce in our lives everything we ask for? No, no more so than good parents are going to fulfill every wish of their children. I will say this: He will do what is best for His glory and for your benefit. "And we know that all things work together for good to them that love God, to them who are the called according to his purpose" (Romans 8:28).

Notes: _____

_____

_____

_____

_____

_____

_____

_____

_____

_____

_____

_____

_____

Shelter in the Time of a Storm

Psalms 46:1-3 (NIV)

[1]God is our refuge and strength, an ever-present help in trouble. [2]Therefore, we will not fear, though the earth give way and the mountains fall into the heart of the sea, [3]though its waters roar and foam and the mountains quake with their surging.

A refuge is a shelter protection from danger or trouble or a place that provides shelter or protection. Strength is defined as the quality or state of being physically strong or the ability to resist being moved or broken by force. The KJV says, "God is our refuge and strength, a very present help in trouble."

I love this verse of Scripture in Psalm 46:1. In the past, I have really depended on this Scripture. When I recite it, I make it personal. *"God is my refuge and my strength, He is a very present help in trouble."*

The world is a dangerous place. People can create painful issues in the cities, and even nature can cause havoc in our lives. There is nowhere that we can escape the chance of being hurt, but the Psalmist gives us a ray of hope—those who look to God in the midst of their pain find a way to get through the rough realities of a fallen world or a deceased loved one. God can give us strength in the time of trouble and times of sorrow. He can create the counterbalance to fear; even when it seems like the earth around us is falling apart.

Verse 1: Hide in Him

"God is our refuge and strength, a very present help in trouble." The Hebrew word "trouble" that is used means "pressed in, confined in a tight space." Do you remember the old saying, "between a rock and a hard place?"

I believe that is the kind of pressure the psalmist is talking about. When life presses in upon us, when trouble comes, then we can know that we have a place to run to. God is our refuge and strength.

It does not matter what form the trouble takes, or how it is delivered, or how long it stays. God alone is our accessible, protected place of refuge and retreat. We can hide there and know that nothing can get through to us unless it goes through Him first.

I'm sure some of us know people who may depend on bank accounts, jobs, families, or relationships. But our God is a far better refuge than any of those. It is not that relationship we've invested so much time in that is our refuge and strength. It is not a job or a house that is our ever-present help in time of trouble.

It is not the economy that gives us our strength. It is not the age, appearance, condition, or health of our bodies that provides us help. It is God who provides us with a place to run, a place to hide. Deuteronomy 33:27 contains this awesome, encouraging truth: "The eternal God is thy **refuge**, and underneath are the everlasting arms."

Psalm 57:1: Have mercy on me, O God, have mercy on me, for in you my soul takes refuge. I will take refuge in the shadow of your wings until the disaster has passed. What does it mean to "take refuge?" It means that we hide there. The Scriptures tell us that we can hide in Him.

Verse 2: Trust in Him

"Therefore we will not fear…" The psalmist is talking about the kind of overwhelming violence of emotions so common to all of us. He illustrates this by using metaphors from nature.

He says that he will not fear though the earth give way and the mountains fall into the heart of the sea, though its waters roar and foam and the mountains quake with their surging.

The psalmist probably had plenty of reasons to be afraid. Look at the words he uses here. The word "fear" in verse two is from a word which described great emotional pain, turmoil, and distress. Also in verse two, the phrase "give way" refers to something being changed in such a dramatic fashion that it could be said to have been removed, and something else put in its place. It has totally collapsed.

Then he describes the mountains falling into the heart of the sea, and he uses a word there that describes something which was apparently immovable suddenly being toppled. And so it is that in our lives sometimes, the things we thought we could depend on, the things which were apparently immovable and dependable, are suddenly discovered to be just the opposite. We lean on them, and they give way.

Verse 3: Believe in Him

We see the word "roar," a word meaning "loud." It has the idea of something being shaken or moved in a violent manner so as to crush or destroy, like the waves of the sea beating against the base of a cliff with enough force and regularity that the cliff eventually erodes and falls into the sea.

The word "foam" means, "to boil." It is used in Lamentations 1:20: "See, O Lord, how **distressed** I am! I am in torment within, and in my heart I am disturbed." That sounds pretty violent. It's catastrophic! But, he says, even if that should happen, I will not be overwhelmed with fear. Why? The key to this is found in the first word in verse two: therefore.

What does it mean? It means "on the basis of what was said in verse 1, God is our refuge and strength, an ever-present help in trouble. Let the worst we can imagine come—we will believe. Though life tosses us around, and the things we lean on suddenly disappear—we will believe. Though circumstances are emotional and uncertain—we will believe.

Though the situation would crush any other person, we will believe. Though all our hopes and dreams suddenly wash out from under us— we will believe. Why? God is our refuge and strength, an ever-present help in trouble.

Verses 4-5 Depend on Him

There are times when I feel down because of the circumstances and situations that I go through. "God is my refuge and my strength, a very PRESENT help in times of trouble."

I have learned to trust in the Lord in a new and deeper way, because I know, that God is my refuge and my strength, a very present help in times of trouble.

When we take refuge in God, He gives us supply and strength. He is always with us.

Ephesians 3:20: "Now to him who is able to do immeasurably more than all we ask or imagine, according to his power that is at work within us."

We can pray anytime, anywhere. God knows before we pray. We don't need our prayers launched into space to be heard. Just open up and speak; God can hear. Don't fear, God will work through you. Turn to Him and you will get all the strength you need.

Notes: _____

_____

_____

_____

_____

_____

_____

_____

_____

_____

_____

_____

_____

Give for the Joy of Giving

Proverbs 3:9-10 (NKJV)

9Honor the Lord with your possessions and with the first fruits of all your increase; 10so your barns will be filled with plenty, and your vats will overflow with new wine.

John 3:16 NKJV

16For God so loved the world that he gave his only begotten Son, so that everyone who believed in him shall not perish but have eternal life.

God gave His Son; What are you willing to give?

Psalm 100 (KJV)

1Make a joyful noise unto the LORD, all ye lands. 2 Serve the LORD with gladness: come before his presence with singing. 3 Know ye that the LORD he is God: it is he that hath made us, and not we ourselves; we are his people, and the sheep of his pasture. 4 Enter into his gates with thanksgiving, and into his courts with praise: be thankful unto him, and bless his name. 5 For the LORD is good; his mercy is everlasting; and his truth endureth to all generations.

Give Thanks with a Grateful Heart

Psalm 100 is the only Psalm entitled, "A Psalm of Thanksgiving."

I believe the Psalm is written from the perspective of a worshipper who has come to the temple in order to present their thank offering.

This is a repetition of Psalm 98:4. The original word signifies a glad shout, the kind of shout Jesus received when he rode into Jerusalem on a colt or donkey. Our God should be worshipped by a happy people; a cheerful spirit is in keeping with his nature, his acts, and the gratitude, which we should cherish for his mercies. In every land God's goodness is seen, therefore in every land should be praised.

Psalm 100 is the pinnacle of praise in a series of Psalms that exalts the Covenant Lord of Israel as the great king of all the earth.

We are called to Worship the Lord, Shouting joyfully to the Lord. Such shouting comes from within, from a heart full of joy.

Matthew 12:34 says, "...out of the abundance of the heart the mouth speaks." If it's not coming from the heart, it's not accepted by God.

Remember, we are coming before the Holy Lord, entering into His presence. Therefore, we do so with respect. We do it with an open and contrite heart, having made confession of sins, having repented of wrong, having trusted in Christ. Being in the presence of the Lord the gates and courts of his temple. Do it in church among believers, in prayer.

It is because of the cross of Christ that we can come before God at all with joyful songs that the Lord God will gladly receive. Our songs of praise and worship should come from hearts filled with joy. Our songs should overflow out of the abundance of grace that has been given to us in the cross of Christ and in all the other blessings we receive. Psalm 34:8 tells us to "Taste and see that the Lord is good." Have you experienced the comforting presence of God the Holy Spirit? Have you felt the presence of God in grace or conviction? Have you known the comfort of God through trials and testing?

To serve the Lord with gladness is to be a cheerful giver. God loves a cheerful giver lending a helping hand to those in need, showing mercy to those who are struggling, practicing random acts of kindness, donating to charities, giving to those in need wherever you go – not out of obligation or duty – but out of gratitude for what God has done for you.

A songwriter wrote, *"Let those refuse to sing Who never knew our God; But favorites of the heavenly king Must speak his praise abroad."*

Serving the Lord is our privilege, to serve the Lord in all things. To serve God is to give what you have – your time, talent, gifts, and service – with a joyful heart. Whatever you do for the Lord do it joyfully. God desires that we be so convinced of His tender love, so persuaded He is at work bringing us into His best, that we will have continual joy and gladness in our walk with Him! Moses warned Israel saying, "Because you did not serve the Lord your God with joy and gladness of heart, for the abundance of all things, therefore you shall serve your enemies, whom the Lord will send against you, in hunger, in thirst, in nakedness, and in need of all things" (Deuteronomy 28:47-48).

God is saying to us today, "Be glad and rejoice in what I have already done for you! If you go around moping, murmuring, and complaining, you will forever be spiritually starved and naked, a prey to your enemies!"

God wants us to so trust in His love for us so that we will be testimonies of gladness and good cheer! God has done so much for us; we have to testify and lift Him up. God said if I be lifted up from the earth, I'll draw all men unto me. God wants us to be preachers who are glad at heart, filled with a gladness that is based on truth.

His truth produces a wealth of gladness that flows naturally outward from the heart. Trust the Father, believe His Word about Himself, and see His gladness pour forth from your life.

³Know ye that the LORD he is God: it is he that hath made us, and not we ourselves; we are his people, and the sheep of his pasture. We ought to know whom we worship and why. God made us. He is the creator. We did not make ourselves. Psalm 95:6 reads, "Come, let us bow down in worship, let us kneel before the LORD our Maker." We are His people – He is the Savior. We are His sheep – He is the Shepherd. John 10:27-28, "My sheep hear My voice, and I know them, and they follow Me; ²⁸and I give eternal life to them, and they shall never perish; and no one shall snatch them out of My hand."

⁴Enter into his gates with thanksgiving, and into his courts with praise: be thankful unto him, and bless his name.

The word thanksgiving means more than just the "giving of thanks." It means, "to make confession, to give praise, to make the sacrifice of thanksgiving." When we begin to confess and to praise, our lives become a sacrifice of thanksgiving before our God. It is by these and these alone, that we can enter into His gates.

When we enter into His gates, we enter into a special place in Him. We enter a place of protection, communion, and provision, where no one can pluck us out of His hand (John 10:28). When we enter into His gates, we come into His courts; we enter into His presence, and are seated in heavenly places in Christ Jesus (Ephesians 2:6).

The heavenly place is the Spiritual Realm of God. Those who dwell in this place have risen above their earthly existence and have ceased from their own labors. These have sought the things that are above and no longer do the things that please the flesh. Only those who have left the old nature behind can enter into this special place that God has prepared for man from the creation. If we are to come into His courts, we must have order in our lives. We can be assured of one thing; there will be order in His court.

[5]For the LORD is good; his mercy is everlasting; and his truth endureth to all generations. This sums up his character and contains a mass of reasons for praise. He is good, gracious, kind, bountiful, loving; yea, God is love. He who does not praise the good is not good himself. His mercy is everlasting. The everlasting unchangeable mercy of God is the first motive of our turning to him, and of our continuing steadfast in his covenant, and it shall be the subject of unceasing praise in eternity. Yes, the Lord is good, and his mercy everlasting; so the full perfection of these attributes in a perfect state will call forth praise unwearied from hearts that ever faint.

Give thanks with a grateful heart, Give thanks unto the Holy One, Give thanks because He's given Jesus Christ, His Son. And now let the weak say, "I am strong," Let the poor say, "I am rich," Because of what the Lord has done for us. Give Thanks.

Bless the Lord. Amen.

Notes: _____

_____

_____

_____

_____

_____

_____

_____

_____

_____

_____

_____

_____

_____

_____

_____

_____

_____

_____

_____

_____

Spiritual Encouragement Strengths

2 Corinthians 7:6-7 (NLT)

[6]But God, who encourages those who are discouraged, encouraged us by the arrival of Titus. [7]His presence was a joy, but so was the news he brought of the encouragement he received from you. When he told us how much you long to see me, and how sorry you are for what happened, and how loyal you are to me, I was filled with joy!

Did you know that even the Apostle Paul knew what it was to feel down? Some people tend to think that Christians should never get discouraged. Somehow feeling very bad without hope is always a sin. If the Apostle Paul was a prototype of what Christians should be, then he should never have been downcast or discouraged. This was not always the case.

While Paul did not spend most of his life as a sad sack, he certainly did have times when difficulties came home to him and he needed encouragement. For example, when he learned about the deplorable situation in Corinth, under the influence of the Holy Spirit he fired off what we have in our Bibles as the first letter to the Corinthians.

1 Corinthians was a very direct and a very hard letter for the Corinthians to receive. Paul pulled no punches in dealing with their sin. Because it was so direct, the Apostle Paul became concerned about how this letter was received and about his own personal relationship with the people who were the church in Corinth. This is why Paul sent his colleague Titus to Corinth to check out the situation.

How do we find comfort when we are down spiritually as Paul was? Paul pointed out three ways in which he was encouraged. He first emphasized that God is the source of our encouragement in 2 Corinthians 7:6. Second, Paul showed how encouragement came from Titus, his colleague in the ministry also in 2 Corinthians 7: 6. Finally, Paul drew encouragement from the Corinthians' response to the truth in 2 Corinthians 7:7.

Although God used others to encourage Paul, the Apostle made sure the Corinthians understood that comfort ultimately came from God. Paul loved to give helpful descriptions of God. I particularly like the one he wrote in **2 Corinthians 1:3**. Before describing some of the dangers he faced for the Lord, Paul wrote, "Blessed be the God and Father of our Lord Jesus Christ, the Father of mercies and God of all comfort."

God, Himself, encouraged Paul. While the Lord was the source of encouragement, Titus, Paul's colleague in the work, was the first means of comfort.

The Corinthians themselves consoled the Apostle Paul on three levels. First, they encouraged him by their earnest desire. We are not told what it was they earnestly desired. It may have been to obey God. It could have been a longing for God Himself. Whatever it was, their desire encouraged Paul.

The second way they encouraged Paul was through their mourning. Again, what they mourned, we are not told. Most likely it was mourning over their sin. Finally, Paul was comforted by their personal zeal for Paul himself.

God delights in helping us when there seems to be nowhere else to turn. What we must remember is that God should be our first option and our last resort. Although not knowing what to do or where to turn is never fun in our lives, God wants to step in and make a way for us in the darkest of night.

What kind of encouragers are we? Do we recognize it as our responsibility to encourage one another? In this self-centered society in America, we forget that God lays responsibility on us to take care of one another in the church. Hebrews 10:24–25 reads, "And let us consider one another in order to stir up love and good works, [25]not forsaking the assembling of ourselves together, as is the manner of some, but [encouraging] one another, and so much the more as you see the Day approaching."

We all walk through difficult times in life. But thanks be to God, Jesus knows all about our struggles, he will guide till the day is done. Thankfully, God provides spiritual resources to help us not only survive these challenges, but emerge from them strengthened and better equipped than ever before.

Hebrews 3:13 tells us to "encourage one another daily, as long as it is called Today, so that none of you may be hardened by sin's deceitfulness." 1 Thessalonians 5:11: "Therefore encourage one another and build each other up, just as in fact you are doing." Throughout Scripture we see instructions to encourage one another and verses that are meant to encourage us. Why is encouragement emphasized in Scripture? Encouragement is necessary in our walk of faith.

Jesus told His followers in John 16:33b, "In this world you will have trouble. But take heart! I have overcome the world." Jesus did not shy away from telling His followers about the troubles they would face. In fact, He told them the world would hate them (John 15:18-21; see also Matthew 10:22-23 and 2 Corinthians 2:15-16). But Jesus' grim forecast was tempered with cheer; He followed His prediction of trouble with a sparkling word of encouragement: He has overcome the world. Jesus is greater than any trouble we face.

Without encouragement, hardship becomes meaningless, and our will to go on decrease. The prophet Elijah struggled with discouragement in 1 Kings 19:3-10, and so do we. It is important to remember Ephesians 6:12: "Our struggle is not against flesh and blood, but against . . . the powers of this dark world and against the spiritual forces of evil in the heavenly realms."

This truth makes encouragement all the more important. It is not just that we face the world's displeasure; we are caught in the crosshairs of a spiritual battle. When we are encouraged in Christ, we have strength to put on our spiritual armor and remain steadfast (see Ephesians 6:10-18). Even in places where Christians do not experience overt persecution or hatred, we all know that life can be difficult.

Discouragement is not an uncommon human experience. At times, recognizing that there is meaning in the seemingly inconsequential things we do seems next to impossible. We may want to give up. Yet He who calls us is faithful, and He gives us the power to be faithful, too (1 Corinthians 1:9).

Encouragement makes it easier to live in a fallen world in a holy way. Encouragement makes it easier to love as Jesus loved (see John 13:34-35). Encouragement gives hope (Romans 15:4).

Encouragement helps us through times of discipline and testing (Hebrews 12:5). Encouragement nurtures patience and kindness (see 1 Corinthians 13:4-7 and Galatians 5:22-26). Encouragement makes it easier to sacrifice our own desires for the advancement of God's kingdom. In short, encouragement makes it easier to live the Christian life.

Without encouragement, life would soon feel pointless and burdensome. Without encouragement the very real pains of our lives can overwhelm us. Without encouragement, we feel unloved. Without encouragement, we begin to think that God is unconcerned with our welfare. So, the Bible tells us to encourage one another, to remind each other of the truth that God loves us, that God equips us, that we are treasured, that our struggles are worth it.

Encouragement gives us the will to carry on. It is a glimpse of the bigger picture. It can prevent burnout. It can save us from believing lies ("sin's deceitfulness"). Encouragement helps us experience abundant life (see John 10:10).

Worship, the Word, and Prayer are three key components to walking in victory when we encounter life's challenges. Used alone or in combination, each contributes to the transforming power of spiritual encouragement.

As you spend time alone with the Lord worshiping Him, meditating on Scripture, and talking to Him, I encourage you as you travel along your journey.

May God bless you and keep you is my prayer. Amen.

Notes: _____

_____

_____

_____

_____

_____

_____

_____

_____

_____

_____

_____

_____

_____

_____

_____

_____

_____

_____

_____

_____

_____

Spiritual Gifts

1 Corinthians 12:1-7 (NLT)

[1]Now, dear brothers and sisters, regarding your question about the special abilities the Spirit give us. I don't want you to misunderstand this. [2]You know that when you were still pagans, you were led astray and swept along in worshiping speechless idols. [3]So I want you to know that no one speaking by the Spirit of God will curse Jesus, and no one can say Jesus is Lord, except by the Holy Spirit. [4]There are different kinds of spiritual gifts, but the same Spirit is the source of them all. [5]There are different kinds of service, but we serve the same Lord. [6]God works in different ways, but it is the same God who does the work in all of us. [7]A spiritual gift is given to each of us so we can help each other.

It has been said, "He who buries his talent is making a grave mistake." How true this statement is for so many Christians. God has given each believer at least one spiritual gift that He wants us to use for His glory, but we often don't use it. We may deny that we actually have a spiritual gift or if we do acknowledge it, we may doubt its usefulness to glorify God, and then just bury it.

But we must realize that God wants us to be involved with His work. He is so gracious that by His Holy Spirit He freely distributes gifts to all who are saved. He not only wants us to *know* our spiritual gifts, but He expects us to *grow* in them each day.

The Bible says in Ephesians 4:7, "But grace was given to each one of us according to the measure of Christ's gift." Also in 1 Corinthians 12:7: "To each is given the manifestation of the Spirit for the common good." Then in verse 11: "But one and the same Spirit works all these things, distributing to each one individually as He wills." So it is clear that each Christian has at least one spiritual gift.

Some may ask the question why we have spiritual gifts. To answer this, let's take a look at Scripture. In Acts 1:8, Jesus says, "But you will receive power when the Holy Spirit has come upon you; and you shall be My witnesses both in Jerusalem, and in all Judaea and Samaria, and even to the remotest part of the earth."

Here Jesus is sharing with us a primary purpose of the gifts of the Spirit: to give the church power in order to preach Christ to the entire world. Preachers are not the only ones to preach Christ. All believers should preach Christ. Paul says another purpose of the gifts is to equip the church for "building up the body of Christ" (Ephesians 4:12). He also reminds us in 1 Corinthians 14:12 that, "So also you, since you are zealous of spiritual gifts, seek to abound for the edification of the church." Therefore, our goal should be to establish, build, and uplift the church with our gifts.

This still doesn't quite answer the big question of why. Why build up the church? For this answer let's again see what the Word says. Revelation 4:11: "Worthy are you, our Lord and God, to receive glory and honor and power; for You created all things, and by your will they existed and were created." Colossians 1:16 says, "For by him all things were created, in heaven and on earth, visible and invisible, whether thrones or dominions or rulers or authorities—all things were created through him and for him."

We exist to glorify God. We were created *by*, *through* and *for* Jesus Christ – to testify of His love, grace, and power. God wants to reconcile with us through His son Jesus, and not only with us, but all His chosen people! That is why we, by His Spirit, are called to be a part of His work on earth. In John 15:8: "By this my Father is glorified, that you bear much fruit and so prove to be my disciples." By bearing much fruit, we glorify God, and we can do this by abiding in Him and using our gifts to serve Him and bring others to Christ.

We are a special part of the body of Christ. If you are a Christian and are not serving in some way, the entire church suffers. It's like missing a part of the body. You may be able to live a normal life with just 9 out of 10 fingers, but you wouldn't be able to do certain things as well as you would like. The truth is, the body of Christ has missing parts. They are attached but are missing in action. The church is called the "body of Christ" for a reason. We are connected by our faith in Jesus Christ and sealed by the Holy Spirit.

Being members of the body, we need to work together. 1 Corinthians 12:12: "For just as the body is one and has many members, and all the members of the body, though many, are one body, so it is with Christ." And in verse 14, "For the body is not one member, but many." Each of us is a specific body part. He also declares that we need each member to function properly as a whole body. He says, in verse 26, "And if one member suffers, all the members suffer with it; if one member is honored, all the members rejoice with it." You glorify God by getting involved.

God wants to use you! He has chosen you for the purpose of doing great things for Him. In Ephesians 2:10 it says, "For we are his workmanship, created in Christ Jesus for good works, which God prepared beforehand, that we should walk in them." God already has plans for you. He wants you to listen to His calling and make yourself available to serve. Not only that, He *expects* you to use the gifts He has given you.

In Matthew 25:14-30, Jesus tells the parable of the talents. It is a parable about stewardship of the grace that God has given to all believers. But let's talk about the servant with one talent. He hid his master's money and was afraid to use it. His talent was taken from him and given to the one who had ten talents. This parable shows us that Christ wants us to use the gifts He has provided to us, not to bury them.

A church can become a graveyard if its members bury their gifts. Instead of burying our gifts let's stir up the gifts. As we get older, we become tired. I have heard some of you say, "I've done my time, let the young people take over." Can I tell you no one is too old to serve God? We must keep growing, maturing, and serving to the end of our days.

To idle away our last years is to rob the church of the choicest gifts God has given to share. There is service to be rendered. There is still much to be done, so let's keep running with endurance. Let's finish the course and finish strong.

Spiritual gifts are also called "grace gifts" and should be valued as gifts of God's grace toward us. We are called to "bear much fruit" that lasts, and our spiritual gifts play a significant role in doing that.

The first step is to pray for God's guidance and ask Him to use you for His will. Ask Him to open your eyes and ears to His call on your life. He will undoubtedly put some direction or calling upon your heart. There are many existing places and ministries to serve in, or He may tell you to start a whole new one! Whatever God calls you to do, be confident that He will provide a way for it.

Discover your gifts. You may already know what your spiritual gifts are. But, if you don't, or just want to clarify what your gifts are, there are both adult and youth spiritual gifts tests to help you find out. Please understand these tests do not guarantee what gifts you have, but they are helpful tools for you to get an idea of how you are gifted.

Try serving in different ministries to see what fits and how you can glorify God in your gifts. God may have given you gifts that you didn't think you could ever have. Or He may transform some of your known talents into spiritual gifts. He will provide gifts for you to accomplish every goal He has for your life.

Our spiritual gifts are to be developed as we mature. Philippians 1:6: "And I am sure of this, that he who began a good work in you will bring it to completion at the day of Jesus Christ." Don't be afraid of what He will do with you. Step out in faith and let Him use you. The rewards will be great.

Be faithful, bold, and humble. Faithfully serve in the small things and allow God to work in and through your life at His pace. Boldly use your spiritual gifts whenever needed, and humbly seek after His kingdom and righteousness.

Be a good steward of your gifts. God says if you are faithful with few things, He will make you a steward over many things. 1 Peter 4:10: "As each has received a gift, use it to serve one another, as good

226

stewards of God's varied grace." Use your spiritual gift or gifts at every opportunity to show the love, grace, and power of God to others. This will produce fruit that remains and will glorify Him.

Use your gifts in love for the glory of God and the building up of His church. 1 Corinthians 13:13: "But now faith, hope, love, abide these three; but the greatest of these is love." Put love into every situation, and every time you serve, may God be the focus.

God bless and keep you is my prayer. Amen.

Notes: _____

_____

_____

_____

_____

_____

_____

_____

_____

_____

_____

_____

_____

_____

_____

Stop Worrying

Matthew 6:25-33 (NKJV)

[25]Therefore I say to you, do not worry about your life, what you will eat or what you will drink; nor about your body, what you will put on. Is not life more than food and the body more than clothing? [26] Look at the birds of the air, for they neither sow nor reap nor gather into barns; yet your heavenly Father feeds them. Are you not of more value than they? [27] Which of you by worrying can add one cubit to his stature?

[28] So why do you worry about clothing? Consider the lilies of the field, how they grow: they neither toil nor spin; [29] and yet I say to you that even Solomon in all his glory was not arrayed like one of these. [30] Now if God so clothes the grass of the field, which today is, and tomorrow is thrown into the oven, *will He* not much more *clothe* you, O you of little faith?

[31] Therefore do not worry, saying, 'What shall we eat?' or 'What shall we drink?' or 'What shall we wear?' [32] For after all these things the Gentiles seek. For your heavenly Father knows that you need all these things. [33] But seek first the kingdom of God and His righteousness, and all these things shall be added to you.

For some of us, not to worry about something is one of the hardest things for us to do especially when the doctor has informed you that you have a life-threatening illness, or you're facing foreclosure on your home, your car is about to be repossessed, your children won't act right, your marriage is about to end in divorce, or any other situation out of your control. As humans we worry even though the Bible tells us not to.

Matthew 6:25 (NLT): "That is why I tell you not to worry about everyday life—whether you have enough food and drink, or enough clothes to wear. Isn't life more than food, and your body more than clothing?" We don't have to worry about that because our heavenly Father knows that you need them. God is a good Father, and He will take care of us if we put him first. We need not worry about human opinion, and we do not need to worry about money and things.

But in Matthew 6:26, Jesus gives the positive alternative to worrying: "Look at the birds. They don't plant or harvest or store food in barns, for your heavenly Father feeds them. And aren't you far more valuable to him than they are?" Single-minded commitment to God and seeking his reign through Christ must be the primary concern of Jesus disciples.

Jesus said to seek first the kingdom of God in His Sermon on the Mount (Matthew 6:33). The verse's meaning is as direct as it sounds. We are to seek the things of God as a priority over the things of the world. Primarily, it means we are to seek the salvation that is inherent in the kingdom of God because it is of greater value than all the world's riches.

Does this mean that we should neglect the reasonable and daily duties that help sustain our lives? Of course not. But for the Christian, there should be a difference in attitude toward them. If we are taking care of God's business as a priority, seeking His salvation, living in obedience to Him, and sharing the good news of the kingdom with others, then He will take care of our business as He promised and if that's the arrangement, why the worrying?

You may ask how do we know if we're truly seeking God's kingdom first? There are questions we can ask ourselves. "Where do I primarily spend my energies? Is all my time and money spent on goods and activities that will certainly perish, or in the services of God—the results of which live on for eternity?" Believers who have learned to truly put God first may then rest in this holy dynamic: "…and all these things will be given to you as well" (Matthew 6:33).

Philippians 4:19 says, "And my God shall supply all your need according to His riches in glory by Christ Jesus." But His idea of what we need is often different from ours, and His timing will only occasionally meet our expectations. For example, we may see our need as riches or advancement, but perhaps God knows that what we truly need is a time of poverty, loss, or solitude.

Our focus should be on pleasing God, on doing his will, on valuing his rewards rather than the temporary rewards of this world. Earthly riches are temporary, and Jesus is advising us to make a better investment—to seek the permanent values of God.

Matthew 6:19-21 reads, [19]"Do not lay up for yourselves treasures on earth, where moth and rust destroy and where thieves break in and steal; [20] but lay up for yourselves treasures in heaven, where neither moth nor rust destroys and where thieves do not break in and steal. [21] For where your treasure is, there your heart will be also."

When this happens, we are in good company. God loved both Job and Elijah, but He allowed Satan to absolutely pound Job (all under His watchful eye), and He let that evil woman Jezebel break the spirit of His own prophet Elijah (Job chapters 1 and 2; 1 Kings chapters 18 and 19). In both cases, God followed these trials with restoration and sustenance. His commandments, His desires, and His love should all be the center of what we are and desire to be.

Jesus was pretty clear when He said to forsake all and follow Him. What He said then, He also means now, even if that means doing things we're not comfortable with, pushing away anything that hinders our relationship with Him, or sacrificing the dreams we want most. Many of us try to ignore how deep and raw this commitment really is. Sure, the Lord wants to give us blessing after blessing. He wants to open every window of Heaven and rain down gifts, both spiritual and natural, into our souls. He wants to fulfill the desires of our hearts. Sometimes we forget, however, that it is humble obedience and faith which bring Him on the scene.

It is always right to obey God right away. God's timing is always perfect. He instructs you to do things at just the right time. God may talk to you through the voice of the Holy Spirit living inside you, through His word, in a dream, or through the authorities He has put over you, like your parents and teachers. When you put off obeying the Lord, you can easily get distracted and forget about doing His will. Then you'll miss out on the blessing that God had in store for you.

If I were to ask, "Which football team is the greatest football team ever?" and I received five different answers, well, that would be okay. Or, if I asked, "What is the best fast food restaurant?" and I received five different answers, that would be acceptable, and maybe even expected. But there is no room for error on the question of our present discussion because the difference between a wrong answer and a right answer is the difference between heaven and hell.

Let's make a commitment not to worry. God knows what we need before we need it. Let's be committed to seeking the Kingdom of God above all else.

Notes: _____

_____

_____

_____

_____

_____

_____

_____

_____

_____

_____

_____

_____

_____

Strong Finish

Hebrews 12:1-2 (NLT)

[1]Therefore, since we are surrounded by such a huge crowd of witnesses to the life of faith, let us strip off every weight that slows us down, especially the sin that so easily trips us up. And let us run with endurance the race God has set before us. [2]We do this by keeping our eyes on Jesus, the champion who initiates and perfects our faith. Because of the joy awaiting him, he endured the cross, disregarding its shame. Now he is seated in the place of honor beside God's throne.

Running the race of life demands a change in our lives. When we accept Christ in our life there must be a change. There is no way we can remain the same.

In order to do something new, you have to change. The reason we don't do new things is because we don't want to change.

Why don't we want to change? Maybe it's because most of us think that we are fine the way we are. After all, this culture tells us that we are to be accepted for who we are, and if anyone does not accept us, the problem lies with them, not with us.

People often make new year's resolutions to lose weight, exercise more, spend less time at work and more time with family, stop talking or texting on the cell phone while driving, etc.

It's not surprising that we want to change the things in our lives that we're unhappy about—even though most new year's resolutions are kept for no more than three weeks.

I believe change is one of the hardest things to do for adults. If we really wanted to change or be a new person and grow spiritually, the first thing we must do is have a change of mind. It all starts in the mind, from your mind to your heart. Running the race of life demands a change in our lives.

Change the way we value God and His word

John 5:39: "You diligently study the Scriptures because you think that by them you possess eternal life. These are the Scriptures that testify about me." You must read the word for yourself.

Change the way you think

Philippians 2:5: "Let this mind be in you, which was also in Christ Jesus." The Bible says that you become transformed by the renewing of your mind. As God changes the way you think, your life will be absolutely revolutionized because it will change the way you live.

Change the way we talk

Romans 12:1: "Now I beseech you, brethren, by the name of our Lord Jesus Christ, that ye all speak the same thing and that there be no divisions among you; but that ye be perfectly joined together in the same mind and in the same judgment." We must talk Godly talk. We can't continue to talk about our brothers and sisters, putting one another down and continue to expect God to bless us.

Change in our level of commitment

Ephesians 4:14: "That we henceforth be no more children, tossed to and fro, and carried about with every wind of doctrine, by the sleight of men, and cunning craftiness, whereby they lie in wait to deceive." **Be committed to whatever you do for the Lord. Proverbs 16:3: Commit yourself to the Lord and your thoughts will be established.**

Change the way we interact with each other

Matt. 7:12: "As you would men do unto you, do also unto them." When there's an opportunity to help someone or share something with someone, we should jump at the opportunity. We must encourage one another.

After change has taken place, we all must be on one accord in order to continue this race and move to the next spiritual level. On the day of Pentecost, the Holy Spirit did not come until they were all on one accord. Acts 2:46-47: "So continuing daily with one accord in the temple, and breaking bread from house to house, they ate their food with glad hearts, [47]praising God and having favor with all the people and the Lord added to their church daily those who were being saved."

Ask God what He wants you to change, improve, or begin to do differently. He might tell you to:

- Demonstrate more of the Fruit of the Spirit in your life, "love, joy, peace, longsuffering, kindness, goodness, faithfulness, gentleness, self-control" (Gal. 5:22-23).

- "Love your enemies, bless those who curse you, do good to those who hate you, and pray for those who... persecute you" (Matt. 5:44).

- "Go into all the world and preach the gospel to every creature" (Mark 16:15).

- "Be content with such things as you have" (Heb. 13:5).

- "Walk according to His commandments" (2 John 1:6).

Whatever He tells you, be ready to act.

As believers we changed into new creations. **2 Corinthians 5:17** tells us, "If anyone is in Christ, he is a new creation; old things have passed away; behold, all things have become new." With that change we can be free from old patterns and failures. We can ask God to help us live each day in the power of the Holy Spirit. Then we can shed the old and embrace the new. Resolutions are easier to keep when we rely on God. It's not how you start the race that counts, it's that you finish.

I'm sure you all have heard Jonathan Nelson's song "Strong Finish."

In this race
That we run
You gotta have endurance
Cause it's a matter of time
I was born sure not to win
In pursuit we came
Until the end

Life's transitions
All in my way
But still I'm onward bound
Each and everyday
No matter what
I'll continue to run
For the rest of my life
Till my work is done

God promised
He'd be with me
Through every step that I take
In this race
By His grace

I'm going to have a strong finish
(Because I have)
Strong faith
I'm going to have a strong finish
(I have)
Strong faith.

We did not enter ourselves in the race. God entered us in the race when he opened our eyes to the glory and grace of Christ. The Christ who died for us and has "destroyed death and has brought life and immortality to light in the gospel" (2 Timothy 1:10, NIV). And God has set his Spirit on us so that we might finish the race (Ephesians 1:13-14).

Wherever you are today – walking or running, stumbling, or limping – if you've wandered or gotten distracted, if you've fallen and are hurting badly, whether it's your own fault or others have knocked you around, it doesn't matter. Finish the Race! Fix your eyes on Jesus and finish the race.

They surround us as a great cloud of witnesses. This doesn't mean that they are spectators of what happens on earth. Rather they witness to us by their lives of faith and endurance and set a high standard for us to duplicate.

The Christian life is a race that requires discipline and endurance. We must strip ourselves of everything that would impede us. Weights are things that may be harmless in themselves and yet hinder progress; they could include material possessions, family ties, the love of comfort, lack of mobility and so on. In the Olympic races, there is no rule against carrying a supply of food and beverage, but the runner would never win the race.

We must also lay aside the sin, which so easily ensnares us. This may mean sin of any form but especially the sin of unbelief. We must have complete trust in the promises of God and complete confidence that the life of faith is sure to win. You must guard against the notion that the race is an easy sprint, and everything in the Christian life is rosy. We must be prepared to press on with perseverance through the trials and temptations. Throughout the race, we should look away from every other object and keep our eyes on Jesus. He is the author and pioneer of our faith in the sense that He provides us with the only perfect example of what the life of faith is like.

He is also the finisher of our faith. He not only began the race but also finished it triumphantly. For Him the race course stretched from heaven to Bethlehem, then on to Gethsemane and Calvary, then out of the tomb and back to heaven. At no time did He falter or turn back. He kept his eyes fixed on the coming glory when all the redeemed would be gathered with Him eternally. This enabled Him to think nothing of shame and to endure suffering and death. Today He is seated at the right hand of the throne of God.

This race is not like any other race. The runners in this race don't have to be swift; they have to endure until the end. Don't be satisfied with just finishing the race, finish Strong. Then you can quote those famous words in 2 Timothy 4:7: "I have fought the good fight, I have finished the race, I have kept the faith."

The apostle wrote these words near the end of his life. These three statements reflect Paul's struggles in preaching the gospel of Christ and his victory over those struggles. So, by declaring, "I have finished the race," Paul is telling Timothy that he had put every effort into the work of proclaiming to all the gospel of salvation.

He had completed the course set before him; he had left nothing undone. He was ready to cross the finish line into heaven. In a race, only one runner wins. However, in the Christian "race," everyone who pays the price of vigilant training for the cause of Christ can win. We are not competing against one another, as in athletic games, but against the struggles, physical and spiritual, that stand in the way of our reaching the prize (Philippians 3:14).

Every believer runs his own race (1 Corinthians 9:24). Each of us is enabled to be a winner. Paul exhorts us to "run in such a way as to get the prize," and to do this we must set aside anything that might hinder us from living and teaching the gospel of Christ.

May we be diligent in our "race," may we keep our eyes on the goal, and may we, like Paul, finish strong. Amen.

Notes: _____

_____

_____

_____

_____

_____

_____

The Call to Worship

During my time of meditation, I thought about the very powerful words in the call to worship.

Minister
Psalm 122**:1-2:** I was glad when they said unto me, let us go into the house of the Lord, our feet shall stand within thy gates, O Jerusalem.

The first thing that we need to know about coming to church is that it is a personal journey. The writer said, "I was glad, when they said unto me." That's personal. Although it talked about others, it says "Let us go into the House of the Lord." I don't care how many people show up; I don't care how many may be in the "us crowd." I understand that this journey of coming to the church should be personal. Church means too much to me personally to allow some other person or some other thing to stop me from showing up on Sunday mornings. From the very first verse, we can sense the excitement, enthusiasm, and the exhilaration of the Psalmist.

People
Psalm 84:10: For a day in thy courts is better than a thousand. I had rather be a doorkeeper in the house of my God, than to dwell in the tents of wickedness.

The Psalmist viewed being in God's presence as much better than being anywhere else. I shared a testimony of a dream I had of being in the presence of God. It was a dream I didn't want to wake up from. The dream was so awesome; I didn't want to share it because I didn't think people would really appreciate it. I don't have time to share the details of the dream now but if being in the presence of God is anything like what I experienced in that dream, those of us who make it will see something so amazing you can't even start to explain.

Minister
Psalm 122:9: Because of the house of the Lord our God, I will seek thy good.

Not because of his own palace, nor because of his own house and family; nor because of his own personal interest; but because of the sanctuary of the Lord, because of the worship and service of God in it. I will seek thy good. The good of the church of God; to do all we can by letting our light shine and stirring up others to do the same. God wants us to be a witness of his goodness, sharing the good news (his word).

People
Psalm 92:13: Those that be planted in the house of the Lord, shall flourish in the courts of our God.

Saints are planted in the house of God; they have a kind of rooting there: but though the church be a good rooting place, yet we cannot root firmly there, unless we are rooted in Jesus Christ. Unless we are planted in the house of the Lord, we cannot flourish in his courts. Unless we are partakers of the grace administered in the ordinances, we cannot flourish in a fruitful profession. **Psalms 1:3:** He shall be like a tree Planted by the rivers of water, That brings forth its fruit in its season, Whose leaf also shall not wither; And whatever he does shall prosper.

Minister
Psalm 26:8: Blessed are they that dwell in thy house, Lord, I have loved thy habitation the place where thy honor dwelleth.

The house here is the sanctuary, which symbolized the manifest presence of the Lord. God dwells in His sanctuary. **Psalm 18:6 (NLT):** But in my distress I cried out to the LORD; yes, I prayed to my God for help. He heard me from his sanctuary; my cry to him reached his ears. God knows everything, sees everyone, and will vindicate the Godly. **Psalm 11:7 (NLT):** For the righteous LORD loves justice. The virtuous will see his face.

People
Habakkuk 2:20: For the Lord is in his Holy temple, let all the earth keep silence before Him.

The temple of God is where God enshrines Himself or allows Himself to be seen and adored. God dwells in His Holy Temple and His presence fills His heavenly Sanctuary. 1 Kings 8:10-11 (NLT): When the priests came out of the Holy Place, a thick cloud filled the Temple of the LORD. [11] The priests could not continue their service because of the cloud, for the glorious presence of the LORD filled the Temple of the LORD. God controls all the earth and expects people to worship him in humble submission.

Minister
Psalm 19:14: Let the words of my mouth, and the meditation of my heart, be acceptable in thy sight, O Lord, my strength, and my Redeemer.

The words we speak are very important. As believers we should not haphazardly say whatever comes to our minds. The Word of God has much to say about our words and how those words affect us. The words of your mouth have a lot to do with the meditation of your heart, the meditation of your heart has a lot to do with the words of your mouth, and both of these can be either acceptable or unacceptable to God. The words of your mouth will have a lot to do with what will happen with the meditations of your heart and the meditations of your heart have a lot to do with what words come out of your mouth. Luke 6:45 NKJV: A good man out of the good treasure of his heart brings forth good; and an evil man out of the evil treasure of his heart brings forth evil. For out of the abundance of the heart his mouth speaks. The meditation of your heart and the words of your mouth can be acceptable or unacceptable to God. It's your choice.

All
Psalm 98:1: **O sing unto the Lord a new song, for He has done marvelous things.** Psalm 98:4: **Make a joyful noise unto the Lord, all the earth sing praises!**

We should always have a song in our hearts, sometimes a new song. David says in this Psalm, "sing a new song." That is, let us put off the old man, and become new creatures in Christ: Psalm 96 1-2 NLT: Sing a new song to the LORD! Let the whole earth sing to the LORD!

[2] Sing to the LORD; praise his name. Each day proclaim the good news that he saves.

In other words, be no more afraid or more ashamed of making a joyful noise and being heard. "Make a loud noise, and rejoice, and sing praise."

When I finished allowing God to speak to me and give me what to say to you, my whole attitude changed forever. When I read or hear our call to worship, I have new life, and I hope you will, too.

May God continue to bless you and keep you is my prayer. Amen.

Notes: _____

_____

_____

_____

_____

_____

_____

_____

_____

_____

_____

_____

_____

Acknowledgements

Great is thy faithfulness
Morning by morning new mercies I see.

Thank you, God, for blessing me and using me to share your word with other believers. Thank you for guiding me through your word, giving what you would have me to share with your people. It is my prayer that you continue to bless me to be a blessing to others through the sharing of your holy word.

Thank you, God, for my wife Evangelyn, who first inspired me to put my expositions in a book. Thank you for blessing us with an awesome marriage of 37 years. Thank you, Evangelyn, for being my best friend, a loving wife, a mother to our children and a loving grandmother. You have always been there for me, encouraging and supporting me along the way.

Thank you, Alfreda Lewis, for being a loving, caring, sharing, and supporting sister – not only to me but to our siblings as well. Thank you for the time and effort you spent in reading and editing expositions to publish this book.

Thank you, Dr. Jessica Wallace McBride, for loving Uncle Ronnie so much that you took time out of your busy schedule to make this book a reality. Thank you for the time and effort you dedicated to getting this book published. I certainly could not have done it without your love and support.

Thank you, Mattie Carter, for following the vision God gave you for the *I Believe Prayer Line*. It is because of your vision the Prayer Line exists. Thank you for allowing God to use you.

Thank you, members of Allen Chapel AME Church, Daytona Beach, and members of the *I Believe Prayer Line* who have encouraged me and supported me over the years. You are a blessing.

Thank you, Reverend Dr. Nathan M. Mugala. You saw something in me I did not know existed. I appreciate the confidence you had in me to allow me to share expositions on the *I Believe Prayer Line*. You are an awesome man of God. Thank you for your leadership and for always being there for me and my family.

To God be the Glory!

Ronald B. Davis

Made in the USA
Columbia, SC
03 November 2022

70336340R00137